# CANADIAN MONSTERS
## &
# MYTHICAL CREATURES

# CANADIAN MONSTERS
## &
# MYTHICAL CREATURES

QUAGMIRE
PRESS

**Andrew Hind**

The Publisher: Quagmire Press Ltd.
Website: www.quagmirepress.com


**Library and Archives Canada Cataloguing in Publication**
Hind, Andrew, author
    Canadian monsters & mythical creatures / Andrew Hind.
ISBN 978-1-926695-37-2 (softcover), 978-1-926695-38-9 (Epub)


    1. Monsters–Canada.  2. Animals, Mythical–Canada.
I. Title.  II. Title: Canadian monsters and mythical creatures.

QL89.H56 2018          001.9440971          C2018-902350-3



*Project Director:* Hank Boer
*Project Editor:* Wendy Pirk
*Cover Images:* dottedhippo/Thinkstock; cosmin4000/Thinkstock;
Rost-9D/Thinkstock; donfiore/Thinkstock; RomoloTavani/Thinkstock
*Images courtesy of:* Cryptopia.us, p. 13; Government of Yukon, p. 26;
Bradley McDevitt, p. 65; *Fate Magazine*, p. 86; Bradley McDevitt, p. 107;
*Le Petit Journal*, p. 138; *Manitoba Sun*, p. 167; Andrew Hind, p. 196.



Produced with the assistance of the Government
of Alberta.

*Alberta*
Government

PC: 32

# Contents

# Dedication

To Claire Anne Hind, who arrived just as work on this book began and who inspired me throughout. You are, and always will be, my greatest creation.

~

# Introduction

~

*The most beautiful thing we can experience is the*
*mysterious. It is the source of all true art and science.*
*—Albert Einstein, "What I Believe,"*
*Forum, October 1930*

Einstein's words remain as valid today as when he penned them more than 80 years ago. Perhaps that's why in the 21st century, despite the fact that the world has become smaller in so many ways and science has advanced our understanding of every aspect of our existence, people seem to crave the mysterious. Ghosts, unexplained phenomena, unsolved crimes, and yes, even monsters, have entered the mainstream and are digested by the public at large.

The term monster is one I use loosely to encompass creatures that may or may not exist. While I think we can all agree that such classical monsters as Medusa and dragons are a figment of our imaginations, are we equally unanimous when it comes to Yeti, chupacabra, Nessie and Bigfoot? The answer is almost assuredly no, as there are a great many people who believe these monsters are merely animals awaiting discovery. There's even a discipline of science, cryptozoology, devoted to researching such anomalies.

Every culture has stories of strange beasts that haunt the edge of civilization. Canada is certainly no different. Indeed, our country has a deep and varied folkloric heritage of mysterious creatures. Many of these monsters originate from the legends, myths and stories of the numerous Indigenous Peoples who lived in Canada first. Others were brought to our shores by early immigrants from all over the world, or developed in recent memory as eyewitnesses have come forward with breathless tales of encounters with something that they've been raised to believe shouldn't exist. Indeed, even as we enter a period in humanity's history where superstition has given way to science and reason, people, with increasing frequency, are feeling empowered to come forward and share experiences that involve so-called monsters.

The accounts of those who have encountered such creatures are typically brushed aside or relegated to fringe media. But lurking beneath these tales are more than a few shreds of doubt—for what if the stories are true?

Such doubts exist for good reason, because one of the greatest fallacies promoted by skeptics is that there can be no major new animals still awaiting discovery in this modern era. To believe we know everything the natural world has to offer, however, is pure arrogance. Indeed, the past one hundred years or so have witnessed some of the most astonishing zoological discoveries of all time, unveiling to the Western world such marvels as the okapi, a short-necked, forest-dwelling relative of the giraffe native to the jungles of Zaire; the largest of the apes, the mountain gorilla; the komodo dragon, the world's largest species of lizard, reaching up to 3 metres in length; the Chacoan peccary, a wild pig from the Gran Chaco region of South America; the prehistoric coelacanth, a fish straight out of Jurassic Park; and in 1976, the megamouth shark, one of the largest species of shark yet discovered. This is to say nothing of the skeletal remains of the so-called Hobbit-man of Indonesia, an evolutionary branch of humanity that co-existed with modern humans for thousands of years.

I think it is safe to assume that there are still more mysteries to be discovered.

I have a deep love for the enigmatic and controversial cryptids that may or may not stalk our Earth. So naturally I jumped at the opportunity to bring some of these mysterious monsters into the public eye through my writing. Hairy hominids. Giant beavers from prehistory. Sea serpents. Colossal bears. These monsters are a varied lot, representing the full breadth of Canadian folklore, from coast to coast to coast. Regardless of their many differences, with a few exceptions the monsters in this book all have one thing in common. Differentiating them from purely mythological beasts, such as the chimera or unicorn, is an uncertainty as to whether these monsters are truly make-believe or are simply rare and elusive (or even, recently extinct) creatures still waiting to be discovered and documented by biologists.

For now, the creatures described within these pages remain strictly relegated to the world of myth and legend, yet compelling accounts exist from people who claim to have actually observed these beasts. And because amazing new species are still being documented, it is possible that in due time some of these "monsters" will earn their rightful place in the annals of zoology.

But even if they don't, it is my hope that you will marvel at the astounding assemblage of mysterious beasts that are said to share this land.

# Chapter 1

# The Thetis Lake Monster

~

One of the most terrifying creatures reported in recent times in Canada is undoubtedly the nightmarish beast known as the Thetis Lake Monster. This humanoid creature is so frightening it appears to have quite literally stepped out of a horror movie, as it is said to bear a remarkable resemblance to the titular monster from the classic movie *Creature from the Black Lagoon*.

Thetis Lake is located in a conservation area of the same name, encompassing 831 hectares of protected forest and parkland about 20 minutes north of Victoria, British Columbia. It has always been a popular spot for picnicking, hiking, swimming, fishing and boating—save for a four-day period in 1972 when visitors were terrorized by a malicious "gill-man" that rose from the weedy depths of the lake.

The first encounter with what came to be known as the Thetis Lake Monster occurred on August 19, a hot, sunny summer day. Two local teens—16-year-old Robert Flewellyn and 17-year-old Gordon Pike—were swimming in the lake when they saw a "spontaneous swelling of water" not far away from where they were splashing about. Seconds later, the surface was broken by a fish-like face with a wide, toothy mouth and horns atop its head. More of the creature's body broke the surface, and now the boys could see that it was humanoid in shape, covered in silvery-gray scales and with webbed hands that ended in sharp, predatory claws. Flewellyn and Pike screamed in fright and ran from the water. A fresh wave of terror swelled within them when they glanced over their shoulders and saw the gill-man giving chase, close at their heels. Close enough, in fact, for one of the boys to receive a nasty cut on one of his hands, either from the creature's claws or the horns atop its head.

The boys managed to make their escape, somehow outrunning their aquatic pursuer. They then went to the local Royal Canadian Mounted Police detachment to report what they had seen. Though the story seemed outlandish, perhaps even preposterous, to the ears of the constables, they duly opened an investigation. "The boys seem sincere," one of the officers told a reporter from the *Victoria Province*, "and until we determine otherwise we have no alternative but to continue our investigation."

The RCMP was still conducting their investigation when the monster struck again. Four days after the first attack, at around 3:30 PM on August 23, Russell Van Nice (14 years old) and Michael Gold (12 years old) watched in amazement as the merman once again rose from the depths of Thetis Lake. According to their description, it was a bipedal reptilian

"shaped like an ordinary body, like a human-being body"with silver-blue scales, huge ears and a horrifying face crowned by six sharp projections atop its head. This time, despite its predatory appearance, the Thetis Lake Monster wasn't aggressive. "It came out of the water and looked around," reported one of the boys. "Then it went back into the water. Then we ran!"

Van Nice and Gold also went straight to the police. Again, the RCMP took the sighting seriously, adding further impetus to the unusual investigation. If something was out at Thetis Lake terrorizing people, the police were resolved to do their utmost to safeguard the public.

On August 26, the RCMP received a call from a man who claimed to be able to solve the mystery. The previous year, the tipster claimed, he lost a pet tegu lizard in the area of Thetis Lake. Tegus, carnivorous lizards native to Latin America, are indeed monstrous in appearance and can grow to more than one metre in length. Case closed? Hardly. The investigating police officers noted this new information, and they considered it for a time before ultimately dismissing the lizard as the source of the hysteria. It simply didn't match the description shared by all four eyewitnesses; the lizard was far too small, wasn't bipedal, lacked ears and its coloration was all wrong. Besides which, zoologists who were consulted were dubious the tropical lizard could endure a Canadian winter.

Nevertheless, the police were eventually forced to close their case when no further evidence emerged, and the creature seemed to simply disappear. Cryptozoologists, however, have kept the file open and continue to investigate.

Loren Coleman, one of the preeminent minds in the field of cryptozoology, made an interesting discovery when he unearthed a bit of folklore that appeared to eerily overlap with the Thetis Lake Monster's description. He found that a similar creature was very much a part of the folklore of the Kwakiutl, a First Nations People native to Vancouver Island. They believed in a fish-like humanoid called the pugwis, which was said to stand about 1.5 metres tall, with sharp fins on its arms and back, wicked claws, bulbous eyes and webbed ears, hands and feet. Most crucially, wood carvings depicting the pugwis show prominent horny protrusions atop their heads—just as eyewitnesses all agree the Thetis Lake Monster had. Tales handed down orally from generation to generation suggest pugwis were frightening monsters but could be kept at bay with fire.

Interestingly, the bizarre episode at Thetis Lake is far from unique. Reptilian man-monsters have emerged from dark lakes and malarial swamps in many parts of North America, all of them eerily similar in appearance to the amphibious "gill-man" of *Creature from the Black Lagoon* fame.

One of the more notorious examples came from South Carolina in 1988 when a flurry of sightings took place. The first occurred around 2:00 AM on June 29, near Scape Ore Swamp, just outside the village of Bishopville in Lee County. On a sweltering summer night, 17-year-old Christopher Davis was forced to pull over on a remote stretch of country road to change a flat tire. The young man had finished his task and was placing the jack and iron into the trunk when, in the pale light of the moon, he spotted something running towards him across an open field.

A lump formed in his throat, and his heart skipped a beat when he got a better look at the rapidly approaching creature: a green-scaled humanoid with a reptilian head and the mouth of a toothy fish. With the gill-man almost upon him, Chris slammed the trunk and jumped inside the car. He tried to close the door behind him, but his horrifying pursuer grabbed hold of it from the other side, gripping the rearview mirror with large, webbed hands. A desperate tug of war ensued, with the panicked teen pulling with every ounce of strength in his body while the reptile-man attempted to wrench the door open. Unable to out-muscle the powerfully built creature, Chris threw the car into gear and pressed down on the gas pedal. The vehicle pulled away in a shower of gravel and dirt, and Chris felt a momentary sense of relief.

Relief rapidly gave way to dismay when he heard something heavy hit the roof overhead, and he realized that the lizard-man had jumped onto the car before it could speed away. You can imagine how terrified he must have been, with only a thin layer of metal between himself and a monster straight out of a horror movie. Thankfully, the creature fell off the racing car.

When Chris arrived home he was trembling with fear and immediately called the local police. Though officers were naturally reluctant to believe such a tale, they couldn't dismiss the proof that was before their eyes: the roof of Chris' car bore a series of long, claw-like scratches, and the side mirror was severely twisted.

The massive media publicity generated by this incident led to many other lizard man reports emerging across South Carolina over the next few months, but few in the decades since.

Needless to say, no real-life creatures of the Black Lagoon variety have ever been proven by science to exist, either during the present or at any point in Earth's past. Yet, if the course of evolution had taken a different turn, our planet may indeed have been home to life forms of this type, at least according to several noted scientists. In 1982, the scientific journal *Syllogeus* published a paper by two respected Canadian palaeontologists, Dr. Dale A. Russell and Dr. R. Seguin from the National Museum of Natural Sciences in Ottawa. Its subject was the fascinating possibility that, if the dinosaurs had never died out, they might have eventually given rise to a dinosaurian counterpart of human beings

In their paper, Russell and Seguin speculated about the likely appearance of such a creature and suggested it would have stood upright on its hind legs, with three fingers on each hand. They even constructed a model of the "dinosaur man"—and in overall appearance it is remarkably similar to the description of the Thetis Lake Monster!

Now, back to Thetis Lake, where the mystery surrounding the monster has only deepened with the passage of time and as fresh eyes look at a bizarre event nearly 50 years in the past.

Daniel Loxton, the Victoria-based editor of *Junior Skeptic* magazine, decided to turn his publication's attention toward the Thetis Lake Monster. His conclusion was there was nothing in the lake back in 1972, save perhaps for mischievous teens who while swimming decided to weave a fantastical tale. Like the police, Loxton wasn't satisfied with the theory that a lizard was responsible. Instead, he noted a strange coincidence that he concluded explains the entire episode. It seems a week before the sightings, a local television station broadcast *Monster from the Surf* (aka *Beach Girls and The Monster*), a low budget horror flick about a gill-man attacking teenagers.

Loxton continued to persevere in his investigation and managed to track down Russell Van Nice, one of the boys involved in the second sighting. Then 49 years old and with the weight of a 30-year-old secret on his conscience, Van Nice confessed that the story "was just a big lie," cooked up by his childhood friend, Mike Gold, to get attention. According to Van Nice, Gold was "famous" for being a habitual liar and telling over-the-top tales.

For Loxton, the case was now closed. He suggested the legend of the Thetis Lake Monster endures only because cryptozoologists continue to write about it and embellish the story with each retelling, giving the story a realism and credence it doesn't deserve.

However, this theory has some problems. In his hurry to stamp "Case Closed" on the Thetis Lake Monster file, Loxton fails to note that neither of the original eyewitnesses, Flewellyn and Pike, have ever come forward to admit that their stories were fabricated. Van Nice and Gold may well have been piggybacking on the published accounts of Flewellyn and Pike for their 15 minutes of fame, but that doesn't mean the original testimony can automatically be discounted. After all, the police believed Flewellyn and Pike enough to open an investigation. Undoubtedly, the police were swayed not only by the earnestness of their testimony but also because one of the boys bore a painful wound (injuring oneself in such a manner seems pretty extreme for bit of local notoriety). Were the teens' memories subconsciously influenced by viewing a B-Movie the week earlier? Perhaps they were. But it seems likely that they saw *something* unusual and terrifying that day.

Then there is the matter of creature from local folklore, the pugwis, which eerily mirrors the description of the Thetis Lake Monster, and the fact that others have come forward in recent years to report encounters with a gill-man in the conservation area. In 2006, for example, a man named Jesse Martin was chased back to his car by a fish-man. The creature lunged at the passenger door and gripped the door handle with large, webbed hands just as Martin was pulling away. Later, he inspected the side door and saw that five scratch marks marred the paint. Further, he saw what looked like fish scales clinging to the door handle.

Despite Loxton's impressive investigatory work, it cannot be said outright that the Thetis Lake Monster has been debunked. Instead, we're simply left with more questions, more layers to unwrap before the truth behind an enduring mystery can be revealed. Until further evidence is unearthed, it's up to each individual to decide: Is the Thetis Lake Monster simply the product of youthful imagination fuelled by a piece of trashy celluloid, or is there something horrifying in the lake—and other lakes across North America—that defies explanation and challenges belief?

As for myself, let's just say I won't be swimming in Thetis Lake any time soon.

# Chapter 2

# Giant Bats

~

With the coming of night, bats emerge from their haunts to take wing…and fly straight into popular myth and legend filled with fear and misconception. For many of us, bats are nightmarish creatures, flying vermin that flitter amidst trees that groan and creak, on wind that makes an eerie sound, like a soft moan of something undead crawling forth from a mouldering grave.

Does mankind have good reason to fear the night? Do giant bats lurk within the darkened canopies of Canadian forests, nocturnal monstrosities with wingspans in excess of 3 metres, whose vampiric appetites are every bit as oversized as their physical form? It sounds preposterous, yet over the past few decades a number of eyewitnesses in southern and central Ontario have reportedly been horrified by the appearance of these fluttering terrors of the night.

The world's only flying mammal, bats have thrived for more 50 million years, successfully living alongside—and indeed, benefitting—humans for as long as we have walked this Earth. One in four mammal species on Earth are bats, and there are sixteen species living in Canada, sadly five of which are threatened due to white nose syndrome (a fungal disease that devastates bat populations while they roost in hibernation) and habitat loss. Of the 1200 bat species in the world, only three are bloodsuckers, all of them found in Central and South America, and even they target only livestock. All of Canada's native species of bats are harmless insectivores, the largest of which, the hoary bat, has a wingspan of a mere 40 cm. In other words, Canada's bats are hardly terrifying.

But what if science is wrong? What if there is in fact a much larger bat fluttering through the darkened skies of our nation? That's a question Liz Butler was forced to ask herself one night in the early 2000s after catching sight of something in her car's headlights. It was after midnight, and the teenager was driving home from a shift at an Orangeville fast-food restaurant. She pulled into the gravel driveway of her rural home in the forested Caledon Hills and slammed on the brakes as something large and black swooped past on dark, leathery wings, captured for a fleeting but still horrifying moment by the beams of her headlights. Liz swears that the creature filled the entire windshield, suggesting it had a monstrous wingspan as wide as a man's outstretched arms. The poor girl sat in the car for long minutes, desperately yearning for the comfort of her bed but too afraid to leave the safety of the car in fear of the threat that lurked unseen in the black skies above. Eventually, she built up enough courage to dash into her house.

There are other eerily similar reports from across southern and central Ontario. In 2002, Dave, an experienced outdoorsman, spotted a "really, really big bat'" flying at treetop height while camping in Ontario's Bruce Peninsula. It was twilight, with the sun just setting over the expanse of Lake Huron, so Dave was able to get a good look at the creature whirling in the gloomy skies above. It flew with the erratic flight typical of a bat, was black, and had dark, leathery wings. He felt certain that the animal's wingspan was at least one metre, perhaps more.

Giant bat tales are not new to Canada. They date back generations. In fact, there's an account from the 19th century that suggests these monstrous bats have been here for quite some time.

In the autumn of 1892, a beast of some sort plagued the tiny Québec village of Ste. Emelie de l'Energie, visiting the sheepfolds almost nightly and carrying off precious lambs. Farmer Joseph Lasalle was determined to put an end to these attacks. Grabbing his rifle, the crack marksman headed off into the woods to confront what he assumed was a hungry bear.

"Some five miles [8 kilometres] back in the woods from the village," reported a contemporary newspaper, "he was startled by hearing a loud croaking cry, and looking upwards he saw, circling high in the air, an immense creature that he first took to be a monster eagle." Thinking that perhaps this was the creature preying upon the village's sheep, Lasalle brought the rifle to his shoulder, took aim and fired. There was a loud crack as the bullet left the barrel, followed by an ear-piercing scream as the monstrous avian was struck. Badly wounded, it tumbled to the earth, crashing through branches and collapsing in a heap in the underbrush.

Though wounded, the creature still lived and continued to squeal in pain. Lasalle shot the creature again and then clubbed the still thrashing beast with the butt of his rifle. Eventually, after what was described as "a terrible struggle," what Lasalle had initially taken for a monster eagle lay still at his feet.

This was no bird, however, as the following description makes clear. "It had two great wings measuring fifteen feet [4.5 metres] from tip to tip. The head, which was fifteen inches [38 centimetres] in circumference, resembled that of a large monkey. The body was five feet [1.5 metres] long, and the back part was covered with a fur or coarse hair. The feet or claws resembled the legs of a wolf...lying with wings extended on the ground, the monster looked as big as a horse, and when weighed was found to turn the scale at 300 pounds [135 kilograms]." Rather than a bird, the monkey-like face and coarse hair or fur sound suspiciously like a bat.

Several of Canada's species of bat are migratory, heading to the southern United States or Central America in the winter, so it's reasonable to assume a hypothetical monstrous bat may exhibit the same behaviour. As a result, it's probably necessary to examine the anomaly of giant bats in a North and Central American context, rather than one limited to the political boundaries of Canada.

The largest wingspan on record for any known species of bat is just less than 2 metres, as recorded for the Bismarck flying fox, a harmless species of fruit bat. The giant bats being described by Canadian eyewitnesses, and fellows in the United States and farther south, would dwarf such a species, being as much as double in size. That alone would make the discovery of a hitherto unknown species of large bat an exceptionally significant zoological find. But there is another aspect that makes the possible existence of the reported giant bat particularly exciting: modern bats are split into two zoological groups—the mega-bats, comprising the large and harmless flying foxes and fruit bats, and the micro-bats, which are small and predatory in nature. Should it come to light that a large, carnivorous bat exists in the forests of Canada and the United States and the jungles of Central America, it would defy our neat categorization and represent a truly groundbreaking zoological discovery.

Giant bats figured prominently in the lore of the Central American Indigenous Peoples, flapping menacingly on oversized leather wings through their collective consciousness. A cult dedicated to a terrifying bat god emerged around 100 BCE among the Zapotec people of southwest Mexico. This god, Camazotz (translated as "death bat" or "snatch bat"), took on the form of a lean man with short-black fur, large membranous wings the colour of coal and a chilling bat head with an upturned nose. The creature's lips were perpetually pulled back in a sinister smile, revealing a mouth lined with crooked, needle teeth, and its eyes glowed red like burning embers of hate. Long arms ended in cruel claws dripping with the blood and gore of a fresh kill. The only clothing the god wore was a bloodstained loincloth made from the skins of recently slain victims. Camazotz was associated with night, death and sacrifice, reflecting societal views of bats as vile, evil creatures. The Zapotec offered Camazotz blood sacrifices in the form of captives to appease his anger and hunger.

In time, the veneration of Camazotz, or Cama Zotz, as he was sometimes known, found its way into Mayan lore as well, eventually spreading throughout most of southern Mexico and into other parts of Central America. The Popol Vuh, a sacred Maya text, identifies the home of Camazotz as Zotzilaha, the "house of bats," a deep cavern located somewhere in the darkness of the jungle interior.

While Camazotz is clearly a mythological character, eyewitness accounts and modern science suggests that the terrifying fantasy of this bloodthirsty creature may have a foundation of actual fact. Some tantalizing evidence suggests that the Camazotz legend may have sprung from a real creature, a monstrous bat larger and more predatory than any species known to modern humans. The Mayans, and the Zapotec before them, so greatly feared this monster that they elevated him to a dreadful god.

Fossil records support the idea of a "super bat." In 1988, a species of fossil bat related to the common vampire bat but more than 25 percent larger was found in Venezuela. This bat, which had a wingspan of almost 2 metres, was named *Desmodus draculae*. Later, another even larger fossil of this mysterious bat emerged from Brazil, suggesting that the animal was widespread and grew to incredible sizes. Clearly, abnormally large bats with a wingspan measuring as much as 3 metres across are a scientific possibility. Incredibly, these fossils date from as recent as 2000 years ago, meaning it's possible that this "super bat" may have co-existed with the early Zapotec people and been the source of their Camazotz legends. In fact, belief in bat demons is widespread throughout Mesoamerica: Hik'al, or "neck-slitter," of Chiapas; Soucouyant of Trinidad, a hag whose many forms include that of a giant bat and Tin Tin of Ecuador.

Some cryptozoologists believe that the monstrous bats, which likely spawned these legends, may still exist, citing reports of giant bat-like creatures that occasionally surface today. While sightings of giant bats are widespread across a huge geographical area, from Canada in the north to Brazil in the south, the greatest concentration comes from southern Mexico, the homeland of the Maya and a heavily jungled region still largely untouched by the advance of modern civilization. Here, descendants of the ancient Mayans adamantly believe that the "death bat" survives to this day. Bear in mind that 2000 years represents a mere blink of an eye in evolutionary terms, and that no large animals have gone extinct save by human hands during this period. If this bat existed two millennia ago, it most certainly could still exist today.

Most anthropologists are quick to say that the monstrous bat is mere superstition, and that the creature of legend is a far more mundane animal made terrifying by skilled storytellers. Some believe that Camazotz and the story of fiendishly massive bats are based on the common vampire bat (*Desmodus rotundas*), a creature that the Mayans traditionally associated with bloodletting and sacrifice. Another suspect is the far larger false vampire bat (*Vampyrum spectrum*), thanks to its greater size and habit of attacking prey around the head or neck. Neither species, however, matches the description of the creature spawned by Zapotec and Mayan myth, still reported to this day. Certainly, neither bat approaches the dimensions of a giant bat, nor would they be frightening enough in size or temperament to terrorize a populace. Could an even larger, unknown species of bat exist in the Americas?

Certainly, there are numerous reports among local tribes of abnormally large bats that attach themselves to cattle and horses, suggesting perhaps the creature from the fossil record still lives today. Research conducted by Dr. E. Trajano, one of the two men who found and studied the Brazil specimen, suggests this is indeed feasible behaviour for *Desmodus draculae*.

Because its appetite must surely have matched its size, he speculates that the giant bat likely fed on larger prey than normal-sized vampire bats, perhaps up to and including humans.

Other stories supporting the existence of a large bat-like creature have come out of the Americas over the last century. In the 1950s, a Brazilian couple was walking through the forest near the town of Pelotas when they saw two bat-winged creatures in a tree. These bats took flight, first landing on the ground, then flying away into the dusk sky, affording the witnesses an ideal view of the shape and dimensions of their wings, and their manner of flight. The creatures were described as humanoids, but their large size and the growing darkness could have led to confusion and misidentification of what was in fact an abnormally large bat species. Interestingly, Pelotas is near where the Brazilian specimen of *Desmondus draculae* was found. Coincidence?

Later, in March 1975, a series of animal mutilations swept the countryside in Puerto Rico. During the incident, Juan Muniz Feliciano claimed to have been attacked by a large, bat-like creature with a wingspan of at least 1.8 metres. This creature was subsequently seen several times during the outbreak; it was always described as having bat-like features, but with a wingspan of 1.5 to 3 metres. Around the same time, a number of sightings of a large bat began surfacing in the Rio Grande Valley of Texas.

These varied reports and careful subsequent research have led some cryptozoologists to assert that some mysterious, as-yet-unidentified winged creature exists in the jungle and deserts of Latin America. In light of the recent discovery of *Desmodus draculae*, might it be possible that what we're seeing is a bat species that reaches monstrous sizes, a creature not born of superstition but in fact part of the natural order?

If this enormous bat exists, it's possible that individuals might find their way as far north as Canada. Certainly, their physiology would be capable of supporting such a migration, and many of our native species migrate south in the autumn. Maybe, just maybe, the eyewitnesses who claimed to have seen giant bats fluttering through the black skies of southern Ontario, and Québec a century earlier, shouldn't have been scoffed at. It's possible that the dark forests of the Americas hide a veritable belfry of giant bats awaiting discovery.

# Chapter 3

# West Point Sea Serpent

~

Old-timers speak in hushed tones of a sea serpent that lurks off the southern shores of Prince Edward Island—a thing created, they say, in the deepest waters of the Atlantic Ocean. For well over a century people at West Point have seen it sliding through the waters offshore, and as a result, the colossal serpent has become known as the West Point Monster. The serpent is the stuff of legend—an obsession for some, a nightmare for others. But does it even truly exist?

Carol Livingstone has no doubt that it does. A lifelong resident of West Point whose roots in the community grow deep and strong, she is certain that something stealthily swims in the waters offshore. She's seen the fear in the eyes of her father and uncle, both of whom claimed to have seen the monster. Their stories weren't tall tales meant to entertain an audience on a terrible night. No, they were a genuine recounting of experiences that left them terrified and questioning all they thought they knew of the world around them.

"My uncle, Stan MacDonald, and a companion, were out on the water near West Point in a low fishing boat sitting, eating lunch," Carols relates. "They felt something looking at them. The thing was looking in the boat. The head would come about three feet [1 metre] out of the water. It was not in the least bit threatening. It was up out of the water with its head raised out. They got a good look at it but had no idea what the thing was."

Ever since people first ventured out to sea there have been monster sightings, and medieval nautical maps often demarked regions thought to be the domain of great sea creatures. The vast and cruel oceans have spawned countless tales of sea serpents. Reports of these creatures are common throughout history, both ancient and modern.

As early as 1555, Olaus Magnus, the exiled Catholic Archbishop of Uppsala, Sweden, attempted to scientifically chronicle sea serpents in his zoological writings. Besides more conventionally recognized marine animals, he said, the coastal waters housed serpents "of vast magnitude, namely two hundred feet [60 metres] long, and moreover twenty feet [6 metres] thick." Even though Magnus' estimation of the creatures' size is surely exaggerated and seems to owe more to folklore than actual observation, we cannot discount his writings out of hand as the balance of his tome is otherwise remarkably factual and forward-thinking for its day.

Some would deride the serpents Magnus describes, and which mariners have been reporting for centuries, as little more than the products of superstitious minds, no more real than dragons, basilisks or unicorns. Those who believe in the existence of sea serpents, however, cite the size and depth of the oceans for the lack of firm evidence, and indeed, marine biologists agree that the vast majority of ocean life remains unexplored.

Of course, sea serpents aren't confined to the Old World. First Nations Peoples have numerous legends of terrifying sea creatures plaguing the waters off North America's Atlantic coast, and almost since European settlers stepped foot in the New World, they've reported seeing mysterious marine beasts that resembled massive snakes, either coiled among coastal rocks or slithering noiselessly through the waters. These creatures have been seen along the entire length of the continent, from the balmy waters of the Caribbean in the south to the frigid, fog-shrouded depths off Newfoundland.

The tiny province of Prince Edward Island is certainly no exception because over the last two centuries there have been numerous reports of sea serpents, especially along the sheltered south shore. The Leard Collection of the Public Archives of P.E.I. contains newspaper clippings dating from the 19th century that recount one fascinating encounter with the West Point sea serpent.

On August 16, 1879, Matthew MacDonald and James Doyle were hauling their trawls in after a day of fishing when they noticed "an unusual commotion in the water near them." Suddenly, the line MacDonald was hauling jolted violently and was torn from his hands with a strength he had never before experienced. He barely had time to register what had happened when "a huge form arose from the sea a full 20 feet [6 metres] out of the water."

McDonald and Doyle were terrified at the sight of the monstrous serpent looming over them. It was like something out of ancient myth, a gigantic serpentine predator capable of capsizing ships and devouring their sailors. The creature's mouth was as large as the open end of a fish barrel, "and each time it raised [sic] out of the water it uttered a roar like the bellowing of a bull." Fearing for their lives, the pair set sail in a desperate attempt to flee. To their horror, they watched as the monster gave chase, slithering with almost supernatural speed through the water.

In desperation, Macdonald tried tossing hake (a type of fish) overboard, willingly sacrificing some of the day's catch in an attempt to pacify the monster, but the ploy only worked momentarily. The serpent ravenously devoured the fish and then, its hunger seemingly unabated, continued its pursuit of the fishermen.

Soon, the slithering monstrosity was overtaking the little boat, its massive maw gaping hungrily. As the creature drew closer, the terrified fishermen could make out additional terrifying details. Doyle said he "counted 12 sharp fins on it, each surmounted with a sort of horn," and both men agreed the colossal serpent was likely 60 metres in length. At this point, neither man thought they would live long enough to relate their experience around a crackling hearth, and while Doyle manned the ship, McDonald hastily fashioned a weapon from a knife fastened to an oar blade with which to defend them. McDonald gripped the weapon in shaking hands, and when their monstrous pursuer came within reach of the boat he lashed out, thrusting with all his strength. The knife's blade sank deep into flesh of the monster's eye and broke off in the wound. The fishermen cheered in triumph as, "with a roar of pain the monster sank out of sight, reddening the water around with its blood."

The next day, their nerves still not recovered from the terror of the ordeal, the fishermen set to repairing their broken lines. Attached to one of the hooks, they found a large tuft of yellow hair clinging to a piece of skin resembling pigskin. This served as evidence to naysayers who thought the men had fabricated the entire tale or, in a drunken haze, had misidentified a more mundane maritime animal. The skin and tuft of hair was displayed for years afterward as proof of the beast's existence, though sadly this piece of physical evidence has long since vanished.

While it's a brave man (or a foolish one) who seeks to kill a sea serpent, it's believed that a specimen was indeed slain some decades after this first sighting. In the early 20th century, a man who lived near West Point went duck hunting in the wetlands along the coast. He built a blind and settled in to wait for his quarry to come in close enough to be shot. Frustration slowly set in, however, as ducks would come in and then suddenly take panicked flight well before he could get a shot at them.

The man knew something was out there among the reeds, scaring the ducks away. He raised his head over the blind to look and saw a huge snake head poking out from the weeds. Despite decades spent hunting these coastal wetlands, he had never seen anything like it—dark and menacing, a massive serpent that established science said should not exist. The hunter aimed his rifle at the aberration and fired. His shot was true. The creature collapsed, lashing about in agony, and died. The man was so repulsed at the sight of what he'd killed that he ran away and summoned neighbours. They accompanied him back to find the carcass and discovered it was more than 4 metres long and weighed an estimated 135 kilograms. Sadly, history doesn't record what happened to the remains.

There have been a number of reported sightings of the West Point Monster of more recent vintage as well. Around 1980, a sea serpent was sighted in the cove between the West Point Lighthouse and the wharf. It was described as being "the length of two fishing boats, that's 60 to 80 feet [18 to 24 metres], long and dark with a head something like a horse." Then, in 1998, a pair of witnesses watched in silent disbelief as a serpent rose from the water less than 15 metres off shore from the sandy beach at West Point Lighthouse. It was said to have fringes around its snake-like head, like some fishes do, and was black or dark brown in colour. The head was above water for perhaps 30 seconds before the creature dove into the depths again, at which time the witnesses caught a fleeting glimpse of a long serpentine body.

Locals who believe the legend of the West Point Sea Serpent—and there are many—are convinced the creature breeds deep in the Atlantic Ocean and occasionally visit the island's shores, probably following schools of fish. That might explain the relative scarcity of sightings over the years.

Weathered sailors have regaled listeners with tales of the West Point Sea Serpent for almost two centuries. Maybe, just maybe, these stories are more than tall tales meant to pass the time on cold nights. After all, as late as the early 20th century sea serpent sightings were reported in newspapers and argued about in mainstream scientific journals. Maybe these sailors knew something that modern science doesn't.

The mere possibility that the West Point Sea Serpent might be a real denizen of the seas excites and terrifies the imagination. The seas are teeming with incredible life forms. Perhaps there's room for one more

# Chapter 4

# Giant Beavers

~

The first day of spring, 1957, was bright, mild and wonderful. The sun was strong enough to melt the snow by day. The first spring bulbs were poking through the surface of the earth, the first green shoots timidly and slowly appearing. This augury of the coming season added a spring to the step of Mortimer Carter, a young man checking his trap lines in the woods of central Manitoba. He trudged through the dirty snow, pushing through the barren willows and browned reeds that shrouded the banks of the river, his golden retriever happily leading the way.

Mortimer had just finished checking a trap and recalls being disappointed that no beaver had found its way into its jaws, when his dog began barking furiously. He looked up to see what had agitated the dog, worrying that it might be an early-awakened bear or a wolf. The retriever was along the edge of the river, about 6 metres away, the hair on his back standing on end. His gaze was firmly fixed on something in the water or on the opposite bank. Mortimer followed the dog's eyes and was stunned at what he saw.

Across the river, foraging on the fresh spring shoots, was a large dark shape that the youngster initially took to be a black bear. He quickly realized this was no bear, however. Instead, it was a huge beaver, which he estimated was taller than his dog and twice as wide. The boy couldn't believe what he was seeing. In fact, he recalls being scared because, having grown up in the woods and being familiar with all the animals native to the wilderness, he knew what he was seeing shouldn't exist. No beaver grew anywhere near so big. Yet, he was staring at a giant beaver, and it was no more than 30 metres away.

Tales of monstrous-sized beavers, as large and intimidating as a black bear, with incisors the length of bananas, have emerged from deep wilderness locations in Manitoba and the Yukon (and indeed into the United States). Does the idea of a 90-kilogram rodent sound preposterous? It shouldn't, because we know such beasts did once exist. The giant beaver appeared at the dawn of the Pleistocene, alongside the mammoth and sabre-toothed cat, and vanished around 10,000 years ago. The only question is whether it might be possible that some relic populations still exist in remote locations today.

For the skeptics, sightings of giant beavers can be explained away as bears, wolves or moose. Not everyone, however, is sure that the idea of monstrous beavers can be dismissed quite so easily. John Warms, a cryptozoologist and the author of *Strange Creatures Seldom Seen*, has extensively

studied reports of monstrous beasts in his native Manitoba. Over the years he has assembled in his files a number of reports of "bear-sized beavers," as well as sightings of huge beaver lodges that, if eye-witnesses are to be believed, come close to the size of an average house. Warms firmly believes it's possible that a relic population of prehistoric giant beavers might still survive, as yet undiscovered, in the boreal forests of northern Manitoba.

Two species of prehistoric giant beaver once existed: *Castoroides ohioensis* and *Castoroides leiseyorum*, but the latter was found only in Florida so is of little consequence to this discussion. These beavers were the largest rodents ever known in North America, measuring about 2.5 metres long and weighing as much as 125 kilograms. By comparison, modern beavers typically measure about one metre in length and weigh about 18 kilograms.

With the exception of its size, the giant beaver looked generally similar to the modern beaver, even though the fossil records shows that the last time the giant beaver and modern beaver species shared a common ancestor was 24 million years ago. However, the two species had other notable differences, as well. By comparison, the giant beaver's hind feet were greatly enlarged and its hind legs shorter, which enabled the beaver to paddle efficiently around ponds and lakes despite its great bulk. The drawback was that its shortened limbs would have made walking on land difficult. In addition, the cutting teeth (incisors) of the giant beaver, which were up to 15 centimetres long, had blunt, rounded tips, unlike the chisel-like tips of the modern beaver. These incisors were not as efficient at cutting wood, and therefore it is possible that giant beavers did not fell trees to construct lodges or dams (many paleontologists surmise that they did; however, and a possible lodge was discovered near New Knoxville, Ohio, around 1912).

The giant beaver's cheek teeth looked much like those of today's capybara or muskrat, making them well-adapted to grinding the aquatic plants that made up the animal's diet. It is also uncertain as to whether the giant beaver's tail was broad and flattened like that of the modern beaver. Because tails are made of soft tissue that decays, we simply don't know for certain, but the size and shape of their tail vertebrae suggests the giant beaver's tail was relatively narrow, perhaps more closely resembling that of a muskrat.

In other ways, the two species were remarkably similar. The skull structure of the giant beaver shows that, like a modern beaver, it presumably participated in extended underwater activity, thanks to the ability to take more oxygen into its lungs. This means it almost certainly had webbed feet to assist in swimming.

Giant beavers were most abundant around the Great Lakes, in what is now Indiana, Illinois and Ohio, but remains have been found as far afield as Yukon in the north and Florida in the south, the Rockies to the west and along the Atlantic coast in the east. In Canada, most fossil remains have been found in Manitoba (where a skull was found in a gravel pit as recently as 2018) and in Ontario.

Radiocarbon dating of the youngest known fossil leads scientists to believe the giant beaver likely became extinct around 12,000 years ago, the same time frame in which the mammoth died out. As with many of the Ice Age mammals, it is uncertain why the massive rodents went extinct. Perhaps they could not adapt to the changing habitats associated with the periods of rapid climate fluctuations at the end of the Ice Age, or maybe they were outcompeted by other semi-aquatic rodents, like modern beavers or muskrats.

Or maybe they never truly went extinct. Reports of giant beavers in North America are certainly nothing new. One can find eyewitness accounts of huge, even violent beavers that date back centuries. Indeed, the famed fur trader and explorer Alexander Henry "the Younger" made reference to monstrous beavers in the journal he kept. These journals, it should be noted, were written in a matter-of-fact manner and have proved invaluable to historians researching his era in North American history.

In 1808, while travelling with David Thompson from Lake Winnipeg, Manitoba, to Fort Vermilion, Alberta, Henry explored Manitoba's Red River. At the forks of the Red and Assiniboine Rivers—today the site of the city of Winnipeg—the explorer met an Indigenous man who told him a fantastic tale, a tale that he diligently recorded in his journal. Henry wrote:

*A Salteaux, who I found here tented with the Courtes Oreilles, came to me this evening in a very ceremonious manner, and after having lighted and smoked his pipe informed me of his having been up a small river, a few days ago, upon a hunting excursion, when one evening while upon the water in his canoe, watching the beaver to shoot them, he was suddenly surprised by the appearance of a very large animal in the water. At first he took it for a moose deer, and was prepared to fire on it accordingly. But on its approach towards him he perceived it to be one of the "Kitche Amicks" or Large Beavers. He dared not fire but allowed it to pass quite near his canoe without molesting it. I had already heard many stories concerning this large beaver among the Saulteaux, but I cannot put any faith in them. Fear, I presume, magnifies an ordinary beaver into one of those monsters, or probably a moose deer or bear in the dark may be taken for one of them as they are seen only at night, and I am told they are very scarce.*

While Henry's words clearly demonstrate a healthy dose of skepticism, they are important nonetheless for confirming that accounts of giant beavers extend at least two centuries into the past.

In fact, the giant beaver figured prominently in First Nations lore, in particular that of the Northeastern Algonquin people. Their tales tell us that these monstrous-sized beavers wreaked great damage with their huge dams, causing a Native hero, Gluskap, to set out to destroy them. One beaver found its way to St. John, New Brunswick, where it built a dam that was so high that "all the land behind it was flooded." The hero, Gluskap, reached the site of the dam and with a great blow from his axe, he tore it apart at the spot that is known today as Reversing Falls. The beaver fled westward, causing Gluskap to give chase in what became an epic hunt that endured for weeks. Eventually, Gluskap gave up. The beaver, meanwhile, continued its westward flight and made its way to the St. Lawrence River where it built a great dam, which created the Great Lakes. Swimming across these lakes, the monster disappeared forever into the land beyond.

Did the mighty Gluskap drive giant beavers west, to populate remote areas where they may have survived thousands of years in tiny pockets? Perhaps. Take, for example, the account of an experienced outdoorsman named William. While hunting moose, the man trekked into an aspen grove, which he knew was the preferred food source for beaver. He wasn't surprised, therefore, to find numerous stumps with the telltale chew marks of a beaver's razor-sharp incisors. What did surprise him, however, was the size of some of the felled trees. Some were almost 50 centimetres in diameter, far larger than even a colony of beavers working together would tackle. His curiosity aroused, Bill followed the drag marks of trimmed branches to a nearby lake, where the beaver could dine in the safety of the water. Along the shore, the hunter noticed fresh prints in the mud—distinctly beaver based on the webbing and horny pads under the first two claws, which Bill knew beavers use to comb themselves. Again, it was the size that startled Bill. The track was about the same size as his own hand, easily double the size of any beaver track he had ever seen previously.

Was the animal responsible a *Castor canadensis* grown so large as to be considered a freak of nature, or was it a member of a *Castoroides ohioensis* population that somehow outlasted the mammoths and other contemporary species?

Does the giant beaver belong solely to the Pleistocene period or, as some assert, do some continue to dwell in the deep lakes, dense forests and inhospitable swamps of the Canadian wilderness? To this day most skeptics attribute Giant Beaver claims to hoaxes or misidentification. But maybe it's not mere fantasy. Can we ignore First Nations oral history and eyewitness accounts and completely discount the possibility that small groups of giant beavers live on?

# Chapter 5

# Caddy

~

The waters off the coast of the Pacific Northwest of North America are said to be the domain of a massive snake-like sea monster. Though reports have surfaced from as far north as the frozen shores of Alaska and as far south as Oregon, the highest concentration of sightings come from the inland waters around Vancouver Island and the northern Olympic Peninsula, and in particular Cadboro Bay, near Victoria, British Columbia. As a result, the creature was dubbed Cadborosaurus, or "Caddy," in the 1930s by newspaper editor Archie Willis.

This is not a creature born of the Internet, tabloid periodicals or urban legend. Instead, Indigenous pictographs dating back a thousand years or more seem to depict this sea serpent, and it figures prominently in First Nations legend, where it was known as *hiachuckaluck* among the Chinook people

One of the earliest Caddy reports on record comes from the pages of the July 18, 1890, edition of the *Daily Colonist*, a newspaper out of Victoria, BC. Eyewitness S.M. Stewart, a respected businessman who owned a logging company that culled trees from the thickly forested island, passed the story to the paper's editor. Stewart related that he and some employees were crossing the mouth of Howe Sound in a rowboat at about sundown, heading towards his logging camp, when Stewart noticed something unusual in the water about 60 metres away from the rowboat. Unsure what the object was, he pointed it out to his companions.

From a distance it resembled a log, "deep black in colour, straight from end to end as an arrow and about 75 feet [23 metres] long." But something about it was off, something that attracted Stewart's attention, and so he ordered the boat be pointed in its direction. When the boat had drawn within 10 metres, the "log" suddenly sank in the water like a stone, dropping noiselessly from sight. Stewart and companions rowed to the spot where the object had moments before been floating and peered into the ocean. There was nothing there.

Shrugging their shoulders, the men started for camp again. They hadn't rowed far when they saw the same object reappear, this time on the other side of the boat and perhaps 45 metres away. Now more than ever determined to see what it was, the men once again headed towards it. Once more, when they drew near the object dropped out of sight. The boaters barely had time to voice their frustration and confusion before the dark shape suddenly breached the water's surface, its black head massive and menacing. The creature blew a stream of water that drenched them, then began lashing about with a long tail, nearly swamping the boat.

Curiosity turned to terror as the loggers feared for their lives. It seemed the monster was intent on throwing them into the water where, it was imagined, they would be pulled under and devoured in the cold depths of the Pacific. The men turned the boat and rowed for shore as quickly as possible. Panic made them ignore burning muscles and aching shoulders as they plowed through the water. The creature pursued them, easily keeping pace and maintaining a distance of 10 metres. It lashed the water unremittingly, causing the boat to rock menacingly and waves to cascade over its sides. All aboard were soaked, cold and terrified.

Then, just as suddenly as it had appeared, the creature sank from view and disappeared, sparing the men from further torment. Neither Stewart nor any of his men could identify the monster, but all agreed it was no whale.

Less than a decade later, Caddy hit the headlines again, this time in an article that was distributed by the *CPR Press Dispatch* to numerous newspapers from coast to coast, including *The Globe* in Toronto, where the story ran on April 15, 1903. The article related how employees at the cable station at Bamfield Creek, BC, had long heard horror stories of a terrifying monster that lurked in the depths of the Pacific, and had been cautioned by First Nations people to be wary when manning their boats or walking along the log-riddled shorelines. The cable station employees paid no attention to these dire warnings, however, reasoning they were just the folklore of what was, in their estimation, a primitive culture.

The skeptical cable operators changed their tune soon enough. One day, they spotted what looked to be a large clump of seaweed floating in the mouth of Bamfield Creek. Then, to their surprise, the seaweed moved and a horse-like head rose from the mass atop a long, slender neck. What was now clearly a serpentine beast of some kind began moving out towards Barclay Sound, swimming "with the speed of a torpedo boat." The men estimated the creature was between 12 and 18 metres long. At a loss as to what they were seeing, they watched as the creature disappeared around the headland and out into open water.

The serpent was reported to have appeared before another witness several days later. It rose from the deep terrifyingly close to a First Nations man paddling across Barkley Sound. The man was so frightened that he ran his canoe into the break-ers and then fled along the beach to the cable station to seek shelter with the employees there. He said the thing had a head shaped like a horse and its body, 3 metres of which was lifted out of the water, was the thickness of a barrel. "The Indians in the neighbourhood are terrified," reported *The Globe*. So, too, were the cable workers.

In 1983, novelist Hubert Evans shared a personal Caddy experience with Howard White, the editor of the *Raincoast Chronicles*. This wasn't an attempt by a master storyteller to weave a tale that would enthrall a captive audience and garner publicity. Had that been the case, he wouldn't have waited more than half a century, and until he was an elderly man in retirement, to share it. White was left absolutely convinced of Evans' veracity.

In 1932 a neighbour named Bob Stephens excitedly arrived at Evans' ocean-side home and urged the novelist to follow him back to his property. Stephens had been watching something through binoculars that he wanted Evans to wit-ness as well.

Evans raced over to his neighbour's home and was directed to turn his gaze out onto the ocean. It was late afternoon, the water was dead calm, and the setting sun was so low that the water appeared to be a sheet of gold. Evans saw a series of bumps breaking the water, all in dark silhouette and circled with ripples.

"It's just sea lions swimming," Evans said, matter-of-factly. "They run in a line like that sometimes." Nothing to see here, the novelist thought at first.

"That's no sea lion," Stephens replied. "Keep watching."

Stephens was right. A minute or so later, at the end of this series of bumps, up out of the water rose a shaft. "This was all in silhouette, so we couldn't see detail, although the outlines were very clear—up, up, up until it must have been six or eight feet [1.8 or 2.4 metres] out of the water," Evans related to the editor of the *Raincoast Chronicles*. He estimated the shaft was at least 12 inches (30 centimetres) in diameter.

As he explained to White, Evans wasn't ready yet to make the leap to accepting the anomaly as a sea monster. "When you see something you don't know what to make of, you keep trying to explain it by the things you know," he explained. So next he suggested to his neighbour that perhaps it was a log. Sometimes, he knew, a log would roll in the current and a limb would come up.

But this wasn't a log, as was soon made apparent. "Right there as we stood watching, none of us breathing a word, the top end of this shaft began to elongate horizontally, until we were presented with the profile of a head, very much like a horse's in general shape, with eye bumps, nostrils and something in the way of ears or horns. The neighbours down the way said it had stuff hanging down like hair, but I didn't see that," Evans recounted. "I tell you, it was a feeling, watching that head come round as if to look at us. It just put the hair up on the back of your neck."

A year after Evans' sighting, another well-respected witness came forward to say that he too had seen a sea monster off British Columbia's shores. Major W.H. Langley, formerly an officer in the British Army and now a barrister and clerk of the province's legislature, swore to having seen a serpent-like beast near Chatham Island on October 8, 1933. Langley said the creature had a long neck and judged it was "every bit as big as a whale." This was a prominent man in the public sphere who had nothing to gain by coming forward with such a tale, and indeed a lot to lose. His testimony should, therefore, carry considerable weight.

Reports of Caddy aren't merely confined to the deep past. Nearly every summer one or two encounters are reported, leaving no doubt that whatever early eyewitnesses were seeing is still out there. Consider the events of the summer of 1993. On July 14, pilots Don Berends and James Wells were flying a Cessna floatplane when they spied two greyish-blue Caddys swimming together in Saanich Inlet. When the pilots landed their plane on the surface of the water, the two sea serpents swam rapidly away. And they did look like serpents. As they swam away, they flexed their bodies into vertical hoops (rather than solid humps), beneath which the pilots could actually see daylight, suggesting the creatures were slender and serpentine in nature. Some have since speculated that the pilots disturbed the Caddys in the midst of mating.

Five years later, in the summer of 1998, Hugh and Sally Campbell and their daughter also saw a Caddy in Saanich Inlet. The couple was boating with their daughter when a serpent arose from calm late afternoon waters. "My wife saw the water moving and then saw this thing, round and black. It was quite fat, more than a foot [30 centimetres] across. It had stepped fins on its back," Campbell said to the *Victoria Times Colonist* newspaper (July 17 edition). The monster quickly disappeared, but five minutes later his daughter spotted it again. Hugh saw "two dark objects, like coils." Again, it quickly disappeared before Hugh could get a closer look at it. "My wife is 100 percent sure of what we saw. We have all seen other sea life, and it was none of that. It wasn't a seal or otter," Hugh said. "I'm a believer [in Caddy] now."

Sightings of Caddy have been so numerous and detailed over the past century and a half that they have spurred serious scientific study into just what species the creature might be. Two men who took up the mantle are Vancouver biologist Edward L. Bousfield, of the Royal British Columbia Museum, and Paul H. LeBlond, a professor of oceanography at the University of British Columbia, both of whom are accomplished in their respective fields. They devoted years of study to Caddy and put together a composite description of the creature based on the numerous sightings. They found that Caddy is basically 4.5 to 14 metres in length, serpentine, with flexibility in the vertical plane, having a horse-like head, a long neck, vertical humps or loops in the body, a pair of side flippers, spikes on the fluke-like tail, and an ability to swim at speeds of 40 knots (about 75 kilometres per hour).

Does this composite help us identify what Caddy might be? Theories abound. Some have speculated that it might be a zeuglodon, a type of prehistoric whale with serpentine features, or perhaps a massive sea snake in the true sea-serpent mould. Others have put forward that it may be a plesiosaur, the same species people believe the Loch Ness monster to be, or the descendant of some other Jurassic sea reptile. Bousfield and LeBlond don't go out on a limb to actually identify Caddy, but based on behavioural evidence, they suggest that it's possible that females come to the shores of shallow estuaries to bear live young. They also hypothesize that the creatures follow the migratory patterns of salmon, spending much of their time far out at sea but following salmon to shore when the fish engage in their breeding cycle. Further, they also suggest that their numbers fluctuate along with salmon populations, perhaps explaining why the frequency of sighting may ebb and flow.

Both scientists agree that the most compelling evidence of Caddy's existence to date is the so-called Naden Harbour Carcass. In July 1937, the body of a deceased sperm whale brought into Naden Harbour whaling station in Canada's Queen Charlotte Islands was opened up and revealed the carcass of an extraordinary creature. Although the ingested animal was decomposed, it was still very distinctive and was described as being "of reptilian appearance." As surviving photographs later revealed, it was 3 to 3.5 metres long, had a head like that of "a large dog with features of a horse and the turn-down nose of a camel," a long neck and a slender serpentine body with two projections resembling forelimbs and a fringed tail section.

Many who examined this anomaly said it was unidentifiable as any known species, yet the official conclusion was that it was nothing more than the fetus of a premature baleen whale. Sadly, the specimen was lost soon after, but photos of it have been studied by a number of experts over the years, most of whom—Bousfield and LeBlond among them—question the official verdict. Bousfield and LeBlond point to this sample as proof of Caddy's existence.

Skeptics may be unmoved. They suggest sightings of Caddy can be explained away as whales, sharks, sea lions or even schools of fish. However, not everyone is sure that Caddy can be explained away so easily. The Pacific Ocean is big enough to hide many wonders. Why not an aquatic serpent?

# Chapter 6

# Shunka Warakin

~

There's a predator out there, the terror of the prairies, that can tear off a dog's head with a single bite, disembowel a horse with one slash of its teeth and raze a homestead overnight, leaving only blood and bones in its wake. This ferocious and tireless hunter is known as the Shunka Warakin.

Mentioned in both American and Canadian folklore, the Shunka Warakin is said to resemble a cross between a wolf and a hyena, with exceptionally strong jaws and a fearless disposition. According to some translations, the name is derived from a First Nations term meaning "carries off dogs," which is apt because legends say the beast would steal into Indigenous encampments under the cover of darkness, soundlessly kill a dog, and then make off with it without anyone being the wiser. The attack was so sudden, so violent, so final that the dog wouldn't even get off a bark, growl or yelp before its life brutally ended. The only evidence of the attack come morning was blood in the grass.

While some might point a finger at wolves, coyotes or even bears as the culprit behind such savage attacks, others believe that the Shunka Warakin is in fact an animal unknown to modern science, a creature that prowls largely unseen through the wilderness of Montana, Nebraska, Iowa, Alberta and Saskatchewan. Those few people who have sighted the Shunka Warakin are adamant that the creature is no wolf or bear, and indeed every eyewitness asserts it most closely resembles the African hyena in shape and form.

Diane and Roger, of Audubon County, Iowa, had the following startling experience late one summer afternoon in 2015 near the town of Elk Horn. The couple was returning home from shopping and driving down a gravel road in a rural, largely unpopulated area when Roger slammed on the brakes.

"What's that?" he asked, his voice laced with a mixture of fear and astonishment. He pointed through the cloud of dust that had been kicked up by his skidding stop towards a strange animal loping along in the ditch.

"The animal looked dark gray and tan, mostly dark gray, had large pointed ears and a long snout. Its shape was like a hyena, and it ran with a different gait than a coyote or dog," Diane said. The astonished couple watched as the animal ran under a fence and up a creek bed to the top of a hill, occasionally looking back as it fled. It took more than a minute to disappear over the crest, affording Diane and Roger ample opportunity to study it. They claim it had "the body and gait the shape of a hyena," and was unlike anything they had ever seen before—despite decades of living in rural Iowa. It was sufficiently alarming that the couple reported the encounter to the local sheriff, but by the time he appeared on the scene the creature was long gone and there were no tracks to be found, as the ground was too hard and dry.

David, a resident of Dallas County, Iowa, had his own apparent encounter with a Shunka Warakin. He and a companion were sitting at a stoplight when a creature that resembled a hyena ran across the road. "It was about two cars length away from us and I turned my high beams on to see it better. It stopped and looked at us but kept going pretty quick... when it ran it kind of looked hunch backed and its head shape reminded me of a hyena," the man relates, noting it was larger than a wolf ("about the size of a small deer") and appeared to have an injured rear leg that caused a noticeable limp in its gait. The creature disappeared into the night, leaving David shaken and convinced he had seen a monster out of myth.

In his 1997 book, *Trails to Nature's Mysteries: The Life of a Working Naturalist*, Ross Hutchins writes in some length about the encounters his grandfather, Israel Ammon Hutchins, had with the Shunka Warakin 150 years ago on his Montana ranch. The Hutchins family settled the Madison River Valley in the 1880s, and shortly after putting down roots, had encounters with a night-stalking predator unlike any they had previously encountered. Ross Hutchins writes:

> *One winter morning my grandfather was aroused by the barking of dogs. He discovered that a wolf-like beast of dark color was chasing my grandmother's geese. He fired his gun at the animal but missed. It ran off down the river, but several mornings later it was seen again at about dawn. It was seen several more times at the home ranch as well as at other ranches ten or fifteen miles down the valley. Whatever it was, it was a great traveler.*

> *Those who got a good look at the beast described it as being nearly black and having high shoulders and a back that sloped downward like a hyena. Then one morning in late January (of 1896), my grandfather was alerted by the dogs, and this time he was able to kill it. Just what the animal was is still an open question. After being killed, it was donated to a man named Sherwood who kept a combination grocery and museum at Henry Lake in Idaho. It was mounted and displayed there for many years. He called it Ringdocus.*

Ross Hutchins examined the beast and had no idea what the animal was, this despite having a PhD in zoology. He speculated that it may have been a hyena that had escaped from a circus, and indeed the stuffed beast did have more than a passing resemblance to a hyena. However, Hutchins also noted that the nearest circus was hundreds of miles away from his familial ranch, and therefore, he had some doubts about this conclusion.

Unfortunately, qualified scientists did not examine the taxidermy mount—the only piece of physical evidence of the beast that was preying on Hutchins' livestock—before it mysteriously disappeared. As a consequence, the Hutchins story was all but forgotten for much of the 20th century and might have remained an obscure footnote to history had a creature, or group of creatures, resembling the legendary Shunka Warakin not begun preying on livestock in Alberta, Illinois, Iowa and Nebraska. Cryptozoologist Mark A. Hall took it upon himself to investigate the beast and in so doing not only uncovered the Hutchins story but also discovered a grainy photograph of the still-missing mounted hyena-like animal. The creature shown in the old photograph is decidedly unusual and frightening, just the kind of creature you can imagine killing dogs and livestock.

So what, exactly, is the Shunka Warakin?

One popular theory suggests that the Shunka Warakin may be a form of prehistoric mammal called Borophagus, an ancient hyena-like canine that inhabited North America during the Pleistocene more than thirteen thousand years ago. Like the modern hyena, Borophagus had crushing premolar teeth and strong jaw muscles that would have been used to crack open bone. There is debate about whether the animal was a scavenger or a predator, but many paleontologists now believe that Borophagus must have been the dominant carnivore of its time because its fossils are so common and geographically widespread. Carrion feeding alone, they suggest, likely could not have sustained such a large population. Borophagus, therefore, would have resembled descriptions of the Shunka Warakin and been behaviourally similar. More, it was even approximately the dimension, being about the size of a large coyote, though granted far more powerfully built.

But Borophagus isn't the only prehistoric animal that may be behind the Shunka Warakin. Some cryptozoologists suggest the creature may represent a remnant population of hyaenodons (also known as cave hyena) or dire wolves that somehow survived into modern times.

Hyaenodon ("hyena-tooth") is a group of extinct carnivorous mammals from Eurasia and North America, and some species of this genus were among the largest terrestrial carnivorous mammals of their time. Hyaenodon had a massive skull, a neck shorter than the skull, a long and robust body, and a long tail—in other words, very much appearing as a cross between hyena and wolf. The average weight of adult *H. horridus*, the largest North American species of hyaenodon, would have ranged between 40 and 60 kilograms, dimensions consistent with eyewitness accounts of the Shunka Warakin.

The dire wolf (*Canis dirus*, "fearsome dog") is an extinct species of the genus *Canis* that lived in the Americas during the Late Pleistocene period (125,000 to 10,000 years ago). The dire wolf was about the same size as the largest modern gray wolves, thus weighing on average 60 kilograms, and was similar in appearance, though with notable differences. Its jaw, for example, was more powerful, with a much greater bite force, and its head significantly larger, while its feet were smaller. The dire wolf would look similar enough to modern wolves to pass for one at a distance, and especially in the eyes of laypeople, yet be distinct enough to confound even experienced outdoorsmen who might get a closer look, or even kill one.

Others suggest a far more mundane explanation: the Shunka Warakin is nothing more than a misidentified wolf, perhaps one demonstrating unusual characteristics. Misidentification of even iconic, well-known species, such as wolves, can certainly happen. By way of example, there was speculation that a predatory creature shot in Montana in 2016 after killing dozens of sheep was a Shunka Warakin. Though it superficially resembled a wolf, this creature nonetheless showed characteristics that were not common to any wolf species native to the region. It had, for example, orange, red and yellow fur, whereas wolves in the area are a grey, black and brown colour, and physically there were a number of abnormalities that gave it an unusual body shape. Even Montana wildlife officials who examined the 106-pound animal weren't sure what they were looking at.

Many cryptozoologists immediately labeled it the missing evidence needed to prove the existence of the Shunka Warakin, but wildlife officials weren't so sure. In an attempt to positively identify the creature, muscle tissue was sent to the University of California, Los Angeles, where DNA samples were taken and compared with DNA from a Northern Rockies wolf. The carcass itself was sent to the National Fish and Wildlife Forensics Laboratory in Ashland, Oregon, for genetic study. To the disappointment of cryptozoologists, the creature was eventually identified as nothing more than a four-year-old male wolf with unusually coloured fur.

In 2007, the cryptozoological grapevine was sent buzzing with the news that the missing Hutchins taxiderm—Ringdocus—had mysteriously resurfaced after decades in hiding. Better still, it was put on prominent display at the Madison Valley Historical Museum in Montana, where it was labeled "The Beast." Now the public could see this mysterious beast firsthand and decide for themselves whether the Shunka Warikin is a living fossil from the ice age or simply an unusual-looking wolf.

Since then, cryptozoologists, and even many traditional zoologists, have been campaigning long and hard to have DNA tests conducted on the creature. Only a DNA test will conclusively determine the identity of the species on display.

Sadly, these pleas have fallen on deaf ears. It appears the animal is caught in a spider's web of red tape. The stalling point, officially, is that the Madison Valley History Association Museum doesn't actually own the mount; the museum is borrowing the mount from another facility and therefore doesn't have the legal right to allow DNA testing. There's speculation, however, that this is nothing more than stall tactics and misdirection. Many believe the museums are resisting doing any DNA testing because they wish to retain the mysterious allure of the creature. Indeed, both museums may feel some need to not have a test done because they believe it would be a less attractive exhibit

The reappearance of the taxidermy specimen actually only further muddies the water. Many observers believe it's a fake, a modern forgery likely made from a wolf pelt designed to attract attention to a small-town museum. These naysayers point out apparent differences between the original in the black-and-white photo and the modern mount. The original creature looks significantly larger, with the neck and head slightly elevated, not leaning downward. The back in the coloured photos is more arched, with an apparent hump over the front shoulders, and the creature's head in the original seems distinctly un-canine-like, with a mouth that is open at an unusually large angle. Even a casual comparison of the two photographs leads one to conclude there's a good chance they are not the same mount.

As a result, even if the Madison Valley Historical Association Museum would grant permission to conduct DNA tests, it may not be the final word on the subject. Even if those results show it to be a scientifically accepted animal, it doesn't necessarily follow that the Hutchins creature, or the "dog stealer" of Native American lore, is nothing more than a misidentified established animal. The layers of this mystery are many.

Is it possible that an as yet unidentified species of predator exists, stalking the wilds of the Canadian Prairies and the upper Mid-Western United States? Will we one day discover that the wolf-like beast that terrorized Native tribes and early western pioneers does indeed exist? Will we be forced to add the Shunka Warikin alongside the names of North America's large predators—the three species of bear, canids like the wolf and coyote, and the three indigenous great cat species (mountain lion, lynx and bobcat)?

Until we know for certain, perhaps residents of the prairies would be well advised to keep their dogs indoors after the sun sinks below the horizon and shadows stretch across the plains.

# Chapter 7

# The Lake Temiskaming Monster

~

According to some estimates, unknown creatures—monsters—are believed to exist in more than three hundred lakes around the world. Canada may well boast the largest number of these monster-inhabited bodies of water, with dozens of lakes and rivers, from Atlantic to Pacific, that are said to be the hiding place of a range of creatures unrecognized by conventional zoology yet with a long history in folklore and myth.

A horrifying snake, about 1.8 metres wide and 10 metres long, slithers through the waters of Lake Utopia. It was first spotted in the early 1800s, and it's a rare summer that goes by without a boater glimpsing this reclusive water serpent. Lake Tagai, near British Columbia's Prince George, is home to a similar monster, though one that apparently tops out at a slightly less terrifying 3 metres in length. Even more fabulous is the Lake Pohenegamook Monster from Québec. This dragon-like cryptid resembles a giant iguana with a cow-like head, is as long as three canoes and is extremely fast and silent. People have been sharing tales of a dark green, 4.5-metre-long serpent in Lake Duchene since 1880. The Lake Ontario Monster has a lineage that can be traced back two-and-a-half centuries earlier, to 1652, when explorer and fur trader Pierre Esprit Radisson sighted a snake-like creature that was 45 centimetres in circumference, with a tapering head and black coloration.

Although it is neither the largest nor deepest body of water in northern Ontario, Lake Temiskaming is one of the most historic, thanks to its ties to the fur trade of the 17th and 18th centuries. It may also be the most famous, at least as far as cryptozoologists are concerned. For centuries, an enigmatic deep-dwelling lake monster has been reported rising from the depths, pervading the myths of Native peoples, fur traders, settlers and modern boaters. This terror of the deep has been the subject of breathless tales told around crackling campfires and in booze-soaked barrooms for generations. Indeed, there are enough eyewitness accounts over the years to elevate the Lake Temiskaming Monster, or Old Tess as she is affectionately known, from the realm of legend to possible cryptozoological beast.

Lake Temiskaming (Lac Temiscamingue in Québec) is deep, achieving a maximum depth of around 220 metres, and large, measuring about 190 square kilometres of surface area. The lake, which lies in Ontario and borders on Québec, lies at the headwaters of the Ottawa River and was, prior to the arrival of railways, the main transportation route in northeastern Ontario. The history of the lake, named by the Algonquians for "deep water," is mixed with Native Peoples, fur traders, loggers, miners, prospectors and settlers. It's also steeped in lore involving a monstrous beast lurking within its almost fathomless depths.

Perhaps the earliest recorded sighting of Old Tess came courtesy of Kate Ardtree. In 1982, the aged woman agreed to an interview from her nursing home with a reporter eager to track down the origins of the Lake Temiskaming Monster. When asked whether she knew anything about the creature, she replied, "Sure I know about it, or should I say them. I well remember my daddy talking about the monster when I was a little girl." These memories would have reached back to the 1910s, when communities like Cobalt, Haileybury and New Liskeard were still in their infancy.

Mrs. Ardtree recalled one day in particular, when her father brought home a scale that he claimed was shed by the lake monster. It looked like a snake scale but was the size of a big saucer, which suggested that her father's insistence the creature grew as long as "two canoes" was no exaggeration. The family kept the scale around the home for years, but it eventually disappeared.

"I wouldn't be surprised if there was more than one monster, perhaps a family of them," she told the reporter. "My dad suspected they must live off Dawson's Point. He used to say there was a crack in the lake bed there and a deep underground river flowing through it." It being winter at the time the interview was conducted, Ardtree warned the reporter to tell readers to keep their eyes on air-holes and pressure ridges on the frozen lake, indicating "that's where Tess used to come up in the old days."

There are more early accounts. In a 1995 interview for the *Temiskaming Speaker*, then 83-year-old John Cobb recalled an event that took place in the early 1940s. Cobb was a life-long mariner, spending decades on the tugboats towing logs across the lake from the White River and Quinize River to the waiting sawmills in Temiskaming at the lake's southern extremity. He was the kind of man, therefore, unlikely to mis-identify any animal native to the lake. That adds an extra level of credence to what he claims to have seen from the rails of the tugboat.

"One night I was coming up [from below deck] just about dark and I see the darn thing in the lake," he recalled. The "thing" he saw in the waters was unlike anything he had ever witnessed in all his life. It was about 6 metres long, with a round head and nose like that of a horse, with dark scales on a serpentine body. "I didn't know what it was. When we come up close [to get a better look] it disappeared." Cobb recalled that other crewmen were as perplexed by the sighting as he had been.

Twenty years later, a youngster named Chuck Coull had an experience of his own while out on the lake. He was boating with his father, enjoying a fine summer day, when they came upon something floating. At first, they thought it was nothing more than a deadhead log. It was dark, slick and shining with moisture, long and thin, almost as long as their boat. As Coull's father drew up alongside it, the "log" suddenly rolled over and began to swim away, at first on the surface and then slowly diving into the depths of the lake. This was no sturgeon, nor a beaver or otter, nor anything else even remotely identifiable. Coull had heard stories of the Lake Temiskaming Monster all his life but had always thought them to be little more than tall-tales. Now he knew different.

A smattering of stories surfaced over the next twenty years before a flurry of sightings in the late 1970s and early 1980s that brought the reclusive creature its greatest attention. New Liskeard Mayor Jack Dent helped cast the spotlight on Old Tess when he spoke to a reporter at the *North Bay Nugget* about the creature and its origins in Indigenous lore. According to Dent, the Indigenous Peoples called the Lake Temiskaming Monster Mugwump, which he claimed means "fearless sturgeon," in honour of its aggressive, occasionally predatory temperament. According to the legend, which had been related to him years earlier by an aging Indigenous person, the creature was the length of "four Indian braves," meaning it was probably in excess of 6 metres.

Not long afterwards, local papers began to dig into the story and search out individuals with their own eyewitness accounts to share with readers. Readers eagerly read the articles that followed, revelling in the fact that their lake might have a monster to call its own, much like Scotland's Loch Ness, Vermont's Lake Champlain, and BC's Okanagan Lake.

The *Temiskaming Speaker* reported in 1978 that Ernie Chartrand of Haileybury watched the creature for several minutes. He and his wife were dining at the Matabanick Hotel, where they found themselves seated at a table where they had an expansive view of Lake Temiskaming. During the meal, their attention was drawn to something moving toward shore. It was large and black, swam low in the water and moved at an unusually fast clip. "As it neared shore, it did a sudden and complete turnabout and headed back to deep water," Chartrand said. "We noticed the large humped back, with no fin, as it swam away. The darn thing must have been 15 feet [4.5 metres] long." Neither Chartrand nor his wife had any idea

what the creature was, but they knew what it wasn't. It was no beaver, otter, fish or any other animal common to the lake.

In its February 17, 1982, issue, *The Speaker* carried a story entitled "Lake Temiskaming Monster Sighted Again," written by Alice Peeper (actually a pseudonym for a woman named Ada Arney). The fact that Arney wrote under a pseudonym and was a known fiction writer has caused many to dismiss this account and others she subsequently recounted in follow-up stories. This is a mistake. The eyewitnesses swore by their statements both at the time and in later years, and as a result, their accounts should not be considered suspect.

The February 1982 story related the experiences of Cobalt-residents, Roger Lapointe and Dan Arney. The two friends were avid ice-fishers, but after the experiences as told in the article both men agreed it would be a long time before they would indulge in their hobby again.

The story begins innocently enough, with the two men borrowing a friend's ice-fishing hut for a night. Lapointe and Arney rode their snowmobiles out onto the frozen surface of Lake Temiskaming and had just settled in after drilling a fresh hole in the ice when their tip-ups started to agitate in an alarming manner. The lines weren't merely being nibbled at; they were being pulled violently by something clearly large and strong. Thinking perhaps they had hooked a large fish, the men hauled the lines in, only to be shocked to discover the bait and lures missing. It looked like they were sheared right off.

Confused but not yet alarmed, Lapointe and Arney reset the lines. They settled back into chairs with steaming mugs of coffee in hand, pondering what was stirring in the depths of the lake below the fish hut. "Probably a sturgeon," the men agreed. No sooner had they come to that conclusion than their tackle was violently pulled down the hole. Eyes grew wide! They had never seen any fish, no matter how big, do that! The men were dumbfounded.

"To hell with this," the frightened Lapointe said to his friend. "Let's pack it in." Arney enthusiastically agreed. He didn't want to linger out on the ice any longer than necessary. The men were throwing on their parkas when Arney said he could feel the small hairs on the back of his neck stiffen. A veteran of the RCMP, he had developed a sixth sense alerting him to danger and when something was amiss. He knew something was wrong and instinctively felt something was watching them. He reached out and put a silencing grip on his partner's arm, and they began to look around the half-dark interior of the hut. Looking downwards, they saw in the fishing-hole a black, glistening head with protruding eyeballs, and one of those eyes was staring at the men. To Lapointe, the eye looked predatory, as if it were sizing up prey.

"Let's get the hell out of here," snapped Arney. With Lapointe close on his heels, he rushed through the door and into the cold darkness of the northern Ontario night. They leaped aboard their snow machine, revved it into action, and then raced for shore with throttle fully open. It was only after reaching dry land, out of reach of whatever swam hungrily beneath the ice, that they relaxed their guard. Both men were deeply marked by fear and shock. The wind carried eddies of snow across the frozen lake, and all was deceptively peaceful, but they knew there was, is, something out there. It's something they can never forget, a horrific realization that means they can never again look at Lake Temiskaming and see only beautiful blue waters and a sportsman's paradise.

Lapointe and Arney weren't the only ones to encounter Old Tess while ice fishing. John Sheur, a New Liskeard resident, claims to have had a literal run-in with the monster one winter evening. Darkness had fallen upon the landscape when Sheur decided call an end to his day of ice fishing. He was locking up his ice hut when he heard a crunching noise nearby. Knowing he was the only fisherman still out on the lake, he decided to investigate. Flashlight in hand, he followed the sound toward a cluster of huts nearby. Rounding one of the little buildings, he almost walked into a long, dark creature stretched out on the ice, it's serpentine body seemingly coiled around several of the huts. The creature had a head that, in Sheur's words, "looked something like a dinosaur." Its large mouth, lined with sharp teeth, appeared to be busily chewing. The frightened man didn't linger long enough to determine what it was feasting on. He ran, pumping his legs as fast as they would carry him, racing so fast it felt as though his ribs would explode and his lungs burst open in a gory shower.

When Sheur reached shore, he ran panting into the bar-room of a local hotel. He nearly collapsed with exertion, and for a while his breath came so ragged he feared he would never breath normally again. Finally, with concerned patrons and staff huddled around, he managed to calm down enough to relate his story. Most scoffed at the tall tale. Sheur tried to get several men to go out and investigate with him, to prove he was telling the truth and perhaps even identify the beast. He begged and pleaded, but no one was eager to pull themselves away from their drinks to brave the cold on some fool's errand. Finally, if only to get Sheur to stop badgering them, two men agreed to take a look. The creature was long gone, but they did find a mysterious snake-like trail in the snow, slithering from the huts out onto the frozen waste of the lake. They also noticed one of the huts' doors had been forced open.

When word of the encounter got out, a Mr. Harmon of Haileybury came forward to add to the story. It seemed he owned one of the huts where Sheur had seen the creature. He had lost a number of ling and other fish left out in the snow that night. When he first discovered they had been taken, he presumed stray dogs were responsible. Then, after hearing of Sheur's account, he began to think perhaps something far larger, far more unusual was the culprit. The fact that three individuals verified aspects of Sheur's story adds a level of veracity lacking in many sightings of the Lake Temiskaming Monster.

Indeed, sightings became so frequent that for a time in the 1990s there was some thought towards using Old Tess as a tourist mascot or as the basis of an attraction. After all, the Loch Ness Monster is responsible for adding an estimated £60,000,000 to the Scottish economy ever year. Nothing ever came of it; however, and the idea has since been dropped.

Some scoff at the idea of an unknown creature living within Lake Temiskaming, while others are more open-minded. The lake is certainly large enough to support one or more large creatures, whether it is a plesiosaur trapped here when the prehistoric ocean that covered the area retreated or perhaps some other prehistoric aquatic reptile. Some cryptozo-ologists have hypothesized that since Old Tess is almost certainly cold-blooded it might survive for months, perhaps even a year or more, without requiring sustenance by allowing its body temperature to drop. Others posit that because Lake Temiskaming connects to the Ottawa River, which in turn flows into the St. Lawrence, the Lake Temiskaming Monster might be migratory and only sporadically inhabit the lake. This might explain why a rash of sightings occur for a few years and then drop off almost completely for years afterwards. After exhausting the local food supply, Old Tess moves on for a time. It's possible.

An interesting theory has surfaced in recent years: Tessie may, in fact, be an Ichthyostega, a primitive amphibian from the Devonian Period. It's a tantalizing possibility because it would account for those occasional accounts of Tessie leaving water to walk about on dry land. Additionally, as an amphibian, Tessie could go into a state of torpor during the height of winter, as salamanders and frogs do, explaining how it survives in winter once the entire surface of the lake is frozen over.

It's also possible that the creature is in fact a sturgeon, an ancient fish that can reach lengths of 6 metres or more, and weights of over 900 kilograms. Though fearsome in appearance, they are harmless and feed on a variety of invertebrates. Sturgeon have been associated with other aquatic lake monsters across North America and are certainly present in significant numbers in Lake Temiskaming. But every eyewitness over the past century has been clear that they'd seen a reptilian creature, not a fish. It's therefore more likely that sturgeon represent a food source for the Lake Temiskaming Monster and not the monster itself.

And then there are those who believe there is nothing even remarkably unusual inhabiting the lake. Ironically, in an effort to draw attention to the monster, *Temiskaming Speaker* reporter Ada Arney may have done Tessie a disservice. The fact she was a fiction author and used a pseudonym for her bylines has led many to question her motives and the veracity of the accounts she chronicled. As a consequence, a shadow of doubt has been cast over Tessie and her existence, meaning relatively little serious study has been undertaken of the subject.

Whatever its identity, for hundreds of years the creature has terrorized and fascinated the people living along the shores of Lake Temiskaming. Highly reclusive, accounts told by shocked witnesses tell of a barely glimpsed serpent-like beast slithering back into the water or diving into the lake's black depths. The reports are fragmentary, and some dismiss them out of hand, but there have been enough reports by reputable citizens over a long enough span of time to at least make one pause to consider the possibilities. Was that a fish brushing against your leg? Or was it the fin of a predatory beast? Something to think about the next time you go for a leisurely swim in Lake Temiskaming.

# Chapter 8

# Kokogiak

~

For most of his adult life, Edward Marston's grandfather, Arthur, lived a great deal closer to the North Pole than to civilization. What television reality shows would today call a "bush person," Arthur survived by hunting and fishing to put food on the table, and trapping for furs to put some money in his pocket. Such a life was hardly pleasant. Many frontiersmen men like him died from scurvy, starved from poor hunting, froze to death when caught by an unexpected blizzard, or—as with Arthur Marston—were attacked by bears.

Arthur was one of the lucky ones. He survived the bear's deadly assault, if just barely. In so doing, he was able to pass on a remarkable story to his grandson decades later.

Winter descended upon Ontario's far north early that year. The mercury plummeted, and snow fell in a seemingly endless flurry. Soon, the view from Arthur's cabin was of endless white all the way to the horizon. Nevertheless, he headed out into the deep conifer and birch forests almost every day to check his traplines for beaver, fox, weasel and other animals whose furs would bring welcome money.

The assault came during the course of one of these days. It was frightening in its suddenness. The first Arthur knew he was in trouble was when an object in his peripheral vision grew large. Too late, he glanced to his side and saw a huge, dark shape hurtling toward him. It caught him across his head and shoulder. He flew through the air, his world turning to black before he hit the tree trunk and crumpled to the ground.

Arthur took a leisurely journey back to consciousness, eventually raising a hand to feel a throbbing gash across his scalp. He had to use his left hand, as his entire right torso was numb. Blood flowed freely from a wound that stretched from ear to ear, running down his face and pooling in the snow beneath his head. Slowly, he pried open one eyelid, then the other. His blurry vision gradually focused on the massive brown paws in front of him, tearing savagely at the frozen carcasses of the animals he had already collected from his traps. As his senses aligned, he looked up at the largest bear he had ever seen. It towered over him, a shaggy monster that was all teeth and massive muscles. It dwarfed any bear Arthur had ever seen in his life; he estimated the bear stood close to 1.8 metres and weighed over 680 kilograms.

Sensation was slow in returning to Arthur's legs. He didn't think he could walk, much less run away from the bear, so he did the only thing he could: Arthur closed his eyes and feigned death. The pain he endured was so strong that, despite being utterly terrified, blackness soon overcame him again. When Arthur came to, the bear was gone, leaving only a trail of frighteningly large prints in his wake. Bleeding heavily from the deep wound in his scalp, with a broken arm and shattered ribs, the trapper returned to his cabin on wobbly legs, where he tended his wounds as best he could and fell into bed. When he was strong enough to move, he returned to civilization for medical attention and never again went back to that cabin. His days in the wilderness, living the life of a frontier hermit, were over. The thought of perhaps running into that bear again, and maybe not surviving this time, was a possibility too terrifying to ignore.

Do I believe the story? Do I believe the bear that attacked Arthur Marston was truly as large as his recounting made it out to be? I'm honestly not sure. But I believe Edward. His pale eyes showed no sign of mirth or deception while telling the story, and he has the kind of handshake, strong enough to break bones, that dares you not to take the man at his word.

Stories of preternaturally large bears, called kokogiak or kinik in some Indigenous cultures, date back centuries. Cryptozoologists point to these stories, and recent eyewitness accounts, as evidence that some form of monstrous bear is out there, awaiting discovery.

If the giant bear of legend does indeed wander the recesses of the Canadian wilderness, its most likely identity is the prehistoric and presumed-extinct *Arctodus simus*, the giant short-faced bear. Among the most terrifying predators ever to appear on the North American continent, this bear lived at a time when a number of over-sized predators prowled the forests, prairies and mountains of what is now Canada. But as fearsome as the dire wolf, cave lion and saber-toothed cat undoubtedly were, none would dare stand up to the giant short-faced bear.

And with good reason: The giant short-faced bear was a true monster, a colossal beast that was among the largest mammalian predators to ever walk the Earth. On all fours it would have stood eye-to-eye with a grown man, and when standing on its hind legs it might have reached 3.5 to 4 metres in height, a full 60 centimetres to 2 metres taller than a grizzly or polar bear. Giant short-faced bears dwarfed modern bears in weight as well. Polar bears are regarded as the biggest modern bear species. Adult male polar bears might weigh around 550 kilograms. The heaviest polar bear ever recorded weighed just over 900 kilograms, which would have been the size of a sub-adult giant short-faced bear. The average adult would have reached 1100 kilograms with ease, and one specimen unearthed in 1935 is estimated to have tipped the scales at more than 1500 kilograms.

*Arctodus* was made even more terrifying because it was capable of speeds that belied its massive bulk. With legs longer than any modern bear, it could run as fast as 50 to 70 kilometres per hour, enabling it to chase down prehistoric herbivores. In fact, in light of its speed, scientists at one point gave it the moniker "running bear."

According to modern science, the giant short-faced bear, dire wolf, smilodon and cave lion all vanished from North America around 11,000 years ago. However, some believe the short-faced bear, at least, may have survived extinction, at least in small numbers.

In Inuit lore, the 10-legged bear they call kokogiak or kinik occupies a prominent role in a number of tales. One of the more oft-told stories goes something like this:

Many, many years ago, men of the village returned home wide-eyed and terrified after a day of seal hunting. As they sat around a crackling fire, seeking comfort and solace in its warmth, they told of a monstrous bear, a kokogiak, which chased them off and devoured the seals they had spent the day stalking and killing.

One man who hadn't gone hunting that day was intrigued by the tale he was hearing. For these brave hunters to have been scared off, abandoning the very food the villagers depended upon for their survival, the creature must have been fearsome indeed. He decided to see for himself, and perhaps slay the beast to ensure his people did not go hungry.

The next day he ventured out onto the ice and came to a large hole in the ice where some seal lungs were floating. This must have been the spot where his fellow hunters encountered the bear. The man decided to set an ambush for the bear, certain that the monstrous bear would behave like a polar bear and return to known seal holes to hunt. The man watched and waited by this hole and, sure enough, the head of a gigantic bear surfaced from the frigid depths. First one massive paw, then another reached out onto the ice to pull its massive frame out of the water. The man saw an opportunity and sprang from his hiding place, rammed his harpoon in first one eye and then the other, blinding the bear.

The kokogiak roared in pain, spittle flying from its massive maw. Blood streaked from its mutilated eyes, but the enraged bear was far from dead. Instead, it hauled its massive frame out of the water and, using scent alone, chased the Inuit hunter across the frozen ice field. The man was understandably terrified, fear lending his legs extra speed. He raced across the ice, running faster than he ever had before until his breath came in ragged gasps; his heart pounded like drums in his chest and his legs burned, but he could not shake his pursuer. Then he saw it, his salvation. Ahead lay two towering walls of ice, with only a narrow gap between. He ran through the crevasse, but the kokogiak, following close upon his heels, was too big and became stuck midway, wedging itself firmly between the ice walls. Now helpless, the bear fell easy victim to the hunter's harpoon.

But while this is certainly a colourful story, the Inuit didn't consider it a fable. Instead, it was viewed as oral history, an event that took place not merely in the storytellers' words but in real life. It should come as little surprise, then, that Inuit hunters continued reporting sightings with colossal bears well into the 20th century. In 1932, for example, Floyd Ahvakana and Roxy Ekownna, along with an unnamed third man, saw what they believed was a kokogiak. In addition to being expert hunters and knowledgeable outdoorsmen, their acuity with the northern landscape honed to a razor's edge by a lifetime spent on the harsh tundra and frigid Arctic waters, these men were "elders of the Presbyterian Church and men of undoubted veracity." In other words, their claims were taken very seriously at the time as they had little reason to fabricate such a story, and it is exceedingly unlikely that all three mistook another, more mundane animal for the notorious kokogiak

Since then, there have been many reports of people spotting impossibly huge bears. The *Idaho Post-Register* of Idaho Falls printed an interesting story in its May 15, 1957, edition. The article suggested giant bears were very real, and terrifyingly so.

"Nathaniel Neakok, the mighty hunter of polar bears, has quit scoffing at reports about the great Kinik being seen in this northernmost region of North America. Kinik is the name Eskimos give to a bear they say is too big to come out of the water. Its size varies with the individual story. But all agree he is a monster of great size and strength and appetite," the article begins. "Several weeks ago, Neakok laughed so loudly when Raymond Lalayauk had reported seeing a 30-foot [10 metre] bear that his hearty guffaws echoed and re-echoed across the great, frozen polar wastes. But Neakok isn't laughing anymore. He has seen a Kinik with his very own eyes."

According to Neakok, the bear he saw "was grayish white and only its head was visible as it swam through the water... its head alone must have been five or more feet [1.5 metres] long—and almost as wide." Neakok estimated the bear must have been 30 feet (10 metres) long, far too big to shoot and kill.

"Until now there have been many scoffers in the village, especially about kinik," the *Idaho Post* story continues, suggesting that people were trying to drum up interest among the media and tourists. "But since the respected Neakok added his testimony, the scoffers are strangely quiet. Even fearful. You don't hear much about how the Arctic's strange mists distort distances or size, creating weird optical illusions."

Tantalizingly, there may in fact be scientific evidence that kokogiak exists beyond the realm of folklore. On June 24, 1864, a huge yellow-furred bear was killed by two Inuit hunters in the vicinity of Rendezvous Lake, northeast of Fort Anderson in the hinterlands of the Canadian north. Three weeks later, arctic explorer-naturalist Roderick Macfarlane arrived and carefully examined the dead bear's remains. Its skin and skull were preserved and ultimately reached the Smithsonian Institute, where the creature was duly catalogued.

Inexplicably, curators dismissed the specimen as a grizzly bear and made no attempt to study it. In time, the skull and pelt were virtually forgotten, buried amidst the seemingly endless artifacts in the museum's vaults. It wasn't until years later, in 1918, that naturalist Dr. Clinton Hart Merriam studied the remains and excitedly came to the conclusion that they represented something truly special. Neither the skull's characteristics nor the pelt's hair coloration seemed consistent with a grizzly, or any other known bear for that matter. In Merriam's expert opinion, these features were so different that he decided the mysterious bear may be more closely related to the extinct giant short-faced bear, *Arctodus*, than any modern bear. Consequently, he designated it as a specimen of a totally new species—and genus—of bear, which he christened *Vetularctos inopinatus* ("the unexpected, ancient bear").

But the story doesn't end there. After all, evidence of a new species of bear should have been one of the greatest zoological discoveries of the 20th century. Yet, modern science only recognizes seven species of bear—brown bear, polar bear, North American black bear, Asian black bear, sun bear, sloth bear, spectacled bear and giant panda. So, what happened to Merriam's groundbreaking discovery?

In the years since, most scientists have come to diminish Merriam's work, reaching different conclusions than the early zoologist. Subsequent research into the brown, or grizzly, bears of North America have suggested that the morphological differences noted in *Vetularctos inopinatus* are likely nothing more than individual variation. In other words, the bear Merriam studied is just an unusual grizzly bear. Because there is only a single specimen of *Vetularctos inopinatus* available for study, there's little scientific data with which to refute the claim.

But of course, there are numerous eyewitness accounts and oral history. American newspaperman, outdoorsman and explorer Caspar William Whitney may have referenced the kokogiak in his 1896 book, *On Snow-Shoes to the Barren Grounds*. It's important to note that Whitney was a serious journalist (he was a correspondent during the Spanish-American War and sent back detailed and accurate reports from Cuba) and an experienced, knowledgeable naturalist who owned *Outing* magazine (a publication that encouraged outdoor sporting), edited *Outdoor America* and was a founding member of the Explorers Club. In other words, he was neither a sensationalist given to hyperbole or a neophyte outdoorsman liable to misidentify animals.

In *On Snow-Shoes to the Barren Grounds*, Whitney wrote of an encounter with "a peculiar looking bear, seeming a cross between the grizzly and the polar, and it has this peculiarity, that its hind claws are as big as the fore claws, while its head looks somewhat like that of an Eskimo dog, very broad in the forehead, with square, long muzzle, and ears set on quite like the dog's. It is very wide at the shoulders, and its robe in coloration resembles the grizzly."

A number of questions arise from this report. Was the animal Whitney saw truly a hybrid bear resulting from the breeding of a grizzly and polar bear? While unusual, such crossbreeds are not unheard of. It is therefore possible that MacFarlane's *Vetularctos* was also the product of a grizzly and polar bear mating. We don't know because to date no one has attempted to compare the remains of *Vetularctos inopinatus* to those of any known grizzly/polar bear crossbreeds. Perhaps these rare animals are what First Nations people call kokogiak and kinik. Or, is it possible that in addition to unusual polar bear and grizzly hybrids, the Canadian wilderness does indeed hide the existence of an as-yet unidentified species of colossal short-faced bear?

Sadly, there's a third possibility, one put forward by naturalist Ernest Thompson Seton. A nature writer, wildlife painter and founder of the Boy Scouts of America, he too was an experienced outdoorsman. He believed what MacFarlane found was indeed a new species of bear, but that the specimen MacFarlane recovered was the last survivor—or one of the last—of its kind, an anachronism whose death in 1864 brought the line of *Vetularctos* to a tragic end.

In the search for confirmation of the continued existence of the giant short-faced bear, perhaps we need to look further afield. On Russia's Kamchatka Peninsula, for generations locals have reported sightings of bears much bigger than the typical brown bears that populate this sub-arctic arm of the Eurasian landmass. Known as the "God bear," or irkuiem, this creature is said to have a massive frame and a unique appearance, characterized by a small head and long limbs that result in a distinctive gait.

Zoologist Sten Bergman lent his name to this bear when, in 1920, he examined a pelt said to have come from one of these animals and came to the conclusion that, in his scientific opinion, it was a unique and as-yet unclassified subspecies of brown bear.

More recently, experienced hunter Rodin Sivolobov has taken up the challenge of identifying this mystery bear. Over many years he has collected a number of eyewitness accounts of the irkuiem and in 1987 obtained from Kamchatka reindeer hunters the skin of what resembled an enormous polar bear, but which they adamantly insisted was from this mystery bear. Sadly, it's not known whether the pelt has ever been scientifically studied. Many cryptozoologists have opined that the so-called Bergman's Bear may be a surviving giant short-faced bear that somehow escaped extinction in the remote vastness of the Canadian tundra and forests of Russian Siberia.

Biologists dismiss this notion for a couple of reasons, but primarily because *Arctodus* is a New World species and is unknown in Asia. However, due to the exchange of animals migrating between North America and Asia via the Bering Land Bridge during the last ice age, it is not inconceivable that a population of short-faced bears could have ended up on the Kamchatka Peninsula. We may never know the truth, as most of Kamchatka is closed off by the Russian officials, making scientific study problematic at best.

Back in Canada, we have had few, if any, reports of monster bears in recent decades. We have precious little to go on. So was kokogiak a prehistoric survivor, and if so, is *Arctodus simus* truly extinct? The examples of MacFarlane's Bear and Bergman's Bear show, at the very least, that unusual bears exist out there in the world. Whether they are new species, relic ancient species or simply misidentified known species is another matter. For some, it isn't hard to imagine that a huge prehistoric bear might have somehow eluded extinction.

However, without valid proof, experts generally write off encounters with these bears as poorly guessed measurements, or perhaps only the tall tales of hunters and outdoorsmen. To link these encounters to a living giant short-faced bear, we need solid proof: a pelt, a skeleton, even DNA.

Until that day, we are left with only questions and the terrifying possibility that maybe, just maybe, the largest mammalian predator to ever stalk prey upon our Earth may still exist somewhere out there and that the vicious kokogiak of Native lore is indeed very real.

# Chapter 9

# Kempenfelt Kelly

~

In 1823, David Soules witnessed something in the waters of Lake Simcoe that shook him profoundly. He and his brother James were tending sheep by the shores of Kempenfelt Bay when he saw something surface in the water. "It was a huge long thing that went through the water like a streak," he later noted. He went on to describe it as having "huge fin-like appendages, and being very large and very ugly looking." This was the first detailed sighting of the lake creature that would later come to be known as Kempenfelt Kelly.

Lake Simcoe, located in central Ontario about 65 kilometres north of Toronto, was formed by glacial melt-waters between 5000 and 10,000 years ago. It was at one point part of the prehistoric Lake Algonquin, which covered parts or all of the Huron, Superior and Erie basins. As water levels in this massive inland sea dropped, Lake Simcoe became isolated from the main lake, trapping various aquatic life forms in its waters.

Simcoe is southern Ontario's largest inland lake. While it is dwarfed by the Great Lakes, with a length of 50 kilometres, a width of about 30 kilometres and a maximum depth of 40 metres, Lake Simcoe is nonetheless still a massive body of water. Kempenfelt Bay, at the head of which lies the city of Barrie, is the western arm of the lake and also its deepest point.

Indigenous Peoples had long believed a monstrous creature of some sort inhabited the depths of Lake Simcoe. Their name for it was Mishepeshu, and it was a name they uttered only in hushed tones. They believed Mishepeshu, which appeared sometimes as a horned sea serpent and other times as a horned lynx, to be an angry and murderous spirit, a creature that feasted on human flesh when sufficiently riled. Fur traders, all of whom were experienced woodsmen familiar with the fauna of North America, also reportedly saw this strange creature many times throughout the 18th century. David Soules' account is the first we have on record. It should be noted that Soules was no newcomer to the wilderness; he had a distinguished record serving as a soldier on the frontiers in the War of 1812, and had extensive nautical experience on the rivers and lakes of Upper Canada. This was not the type of man who might mistake a beaver or a moose for a sea serpent.

The creature, as described by Soules and dozens of witnesses since, defies easy classification. It is almost always brown in colour, with a long neck topped by a head resembling that of a dog. The monster has often been described as a slow swimmer, gliding along at a leisurely pace even when in the presence of humans, and indeed seems quite curious by nature, willfully surfacing alongside boats or approaching startled people on shore. The largest specimen sighted was estimated to have been only 3.5 metres in length, much smaller than those creatures reputedly inhabiting Loch Ness or even other Canadian lakes.

While the creature that later would come to be known as Kelly has been seen across the entire length of the lake, from Cooks Bay to the Narrows at Orillia, by far the majority of sightings have occurred in or near Kempenfelt Bay. As it is the deepest part of the lake, it's perhaps natural that a creature attempting to elude discovery would reside in the bay. Local folklore suggests there are underwater tunnels beneath Kempenfelt Bay linking Lake Simcoe to other large bodies of water. This "theory," if we can call it that, would conveniently account for the reports of similar aquatic monsters in these widely dispersed lakes, and explain how a genetic pool large enough to support a viable population could exist.

A flurry of encounters occurred in the late 19th and early 20th centuries. In the 1880s, F.J. Delany claimed to have captured one of the creatures. The *Orillia Packet* provided a detailed account of the event and described the serpent as having "two antennae of great length and sensitiveness...four hooks or grabbers, which make the animal resemble an octopus in front...three pairs of legs....and at the end of its tail are attached three other curious members in a fan-like position, which, it is believed, are used as a rudder." Around the same time reports surfaced suggesting the beast was responsible for the death of sheep grazing along the shores of Cooks Bay. In one episode, a startled witness saw the creature spring from the water and snatch its helpless prey in its mouth, then drag the kill into the lake where it was presumably devoured.

Remember, Native Peoples always held that the creature should be feared.

In the early 1900s, the Carley family operated a boat manufacturing business at the foot of Mulcaster Street in Barrie. Their wharf became a popular spot for viewing the beast. Indeed, during a rowing regatta offshore, Carley was reputedly forced off-course when the creature suddenly surfaced in front of his boat. In 1903, a beast with a "head as big as a dog and with horns" startled a pair of railway detectives who were boating near the Carley wharf. Two years later, three more people saw the serpent in the same vicinity. Around this time, local newspapers began to refer to it as the "C Monster," a playful take on "sea monster" and in keeping with its association with the Carley family.

This name wasn't destined to stick, either. Decades later, it was given the name Igopogo by Wellington Charles, a Native guide, after a sighting that occurred on July 31, 1952. Charles thought the name was appropriate in light of its similarity to other great lake monsters of Canadian lore, including Okanagan Lake's Ogopogo and Lake Manitoba's Manipogo. The creature's current and most common name was adopted in 1967 when Arch Brown, a resident of Oro-Medonte Township, decided Lake Simcoe's resident monster needed a catchier name to go with modern times after seeing the creature four times (Brown described the creature as being 3 metres long and having a dark grey, serpent-like body with a dog-shaped head). He copyrighted the name Kempenfelt Kelly and donated it to the City of Barrie for tourism promotion. Anne Binkley created a now-famous cartoon for the Chamber of Commerce, putting a cuddly and marketable face on the elusive beast.

Sightings continued over the decades that followed. One took place in the shallows of Cook's Bay, when two men—experienced anglers who had spent more than thirty years on the lake—were fishing in 10 metres of water. The water was so clear that the men could see near the bottom. Suddenly, a large black mass swam beneath their boat, completely filling their view. Then, both of their rods began screeching wildly, and lines were drawn out as something took their bait. The rods bent sharply, before snapping in half. "We both looked at each other in disbelief and never spoke of that moment again," the man explained in an online message board.

From the opposite end of Lake Simcoe comes the next perplexing episode. Two brothers were fishing for perch in McPhee Bay on a cool fall day. The men had the lake to themselves; there were no other boats in sight. The weather was calm with barely a breeze, so that the lake looked like a mirror reflecting the fiery fall foliage of the surrounding shoreline. One of the brothers shattered the calm with a startled "What the hell!" His eyes were wide as he watched a 60-centimetre swell coming down the middle of the bay, just like you'd see from the wake of a bigger boats...except there were no other boats. In the absence of another watercraft or wind, and knowing beavers or otter were incapable of making such large swells, the men were forced to conclude they had seen a large, submerged creature of some sort.

Nevertheless, the question remains. Is there really a sea monster lurking in the depths of Lake Simcoe? In recent years there has been some tantalizing evidence indicating there might well be something down there. In 1978, sonar scans of the lake's depths captured large shapes moving below the surface, and on June 13, 1983, William J. Skrypetz caught something on radar from the Government Dock and Marina in Lefroy, the outline of which indicated the presence of a subsurface serpent-like creature.

Possibly the most remarkable evidence comes from a video shot in 1991. A cameraman was videotaping a friend racing his boat across Cooks Bay when the craft suddenly broke down. As the boater began repairs, something quietly surfaced a few metres away. At first, the creature rose up out of the water on a long neck and seemed to consider the boater. Then, it slowly sank back into the water and peered upward with only the top of its head visible above the surface. A few minutes later it submerged and disappeared. Incredibly, the whole episode was captured on film. The quality of the video is excellent, clearly showing an unusual creature of some kind.

Ironically, while believers lauded the film as proof that a previously unknown species existed in Lake Simcoe, it may have only muddied the water. Cryptozoologist John Kirk of the British Columbia Scientific Cryptozoology Club (BCSCC) studied the film and came to the conclusion that it was indeed authentic, but was similarly convinced the creature was a pinniped. In other words, Kempenfelt Kelly was, in his estimation, a seal or sea lion. But one that was truly large in size. It's not as farfetched a notion as it might initially sound. Seals have been sighted in tributaries of the St. Lawrence River, the Great Lakes and various smaller lakes hundreds of miles from the sea. Thanks to its connection to the St. Lawrence system via the Trent-Severn seaway, it is theoretically possible that a pinniped—a seal of some species—could have made its way into Lake Simcoe.

Others have postulated that sightings of Kempenfelt Kelly can be attributed to a relic population of seal or seal-like creature, some prehistoric species that has gone undocumented and remained largely unseen for millennia. Those who adhere to this theory point to two prime problems with Kelly being simply a seal that happened to wander into Lake Simcoe from the St. Lawrence. First, there are the countless recorded sightings of the creature dating back to David Soules in the early 19th century, and before that the folklore of the local First Nations. A lone, wayward pinniped doesn't explain these early sightings. No, the number of sightings over such a long period of time suggests a native population—whatever Kelly might be.

The second problem with the wayward seal theory is the number of sightings of something eerily similar to Kelly in other bodies of water along or near the Trent-Severn Seaway, the 386-kilometre-long canal route connecting Lake Ontario at Trenton with Lake Huron at Port Severn, encompassing the Trent River, the Otonabee River, the Kawartha Lakes, Lake Simcoe, Lake Couchiching and the Severn River. What some cryptozoologists theorize is that the opening of the Trent-Severn Seaway in 1920 allowed a relic population of prehistoric beast that was heretofore largely confined to Lake

Simcoe to now move freely along the length of this waterway, perhaps even spawning new populations in other lakes.

"I honestly feel with no sightings for years that the creature is gone, but the detractors who say that it's an impossibility are also wrong. Unless someone can go over every large inch of that massive lake from Barrie to Couchiching to the Trent-Severn Waterway, and do it every day, there is always a possibility," explains Kirk, noting that Lake Simcoe is "pristine" and "habitable" and "very able to sustain a large array of aquatic life," up to and including a large, undocumented marine species.

Plesiosaur, prehistoric pinniped or common seal—what exactly is Kelly? While the debate over Kempenfelt Kelly's identity continues to thrive, the creature itself eludes us in the depths of Lake Simcoe.

# Chapter 10

# Qallupilluk

~

The boy poured a cup of tea, his breath forming clouds in the air despite his proximity to a hissing stove. Outside, snow piled up against the sole window of the drafty one-room shack and raced in gusts around the yard outside. Normally, the boy found the warmth of a tea mug in his hands soothing, calming, but not today. Today, something felt off, wrong. There was an unmistakable hint of malice in the frosty air.

He heard his father's sled dogs straining at their chains in a tremendous fit of howling, barking and yelping. That caught his attention. Those dogs weren't merely his friends, but they were also his father's means of survival. Without them, he couldn't hunt, trap or make his infrequent trips to the trading post for supplies. The anxiousness, almost fear in their barking sent a shiver down the boy's spine. Something out there was putting the dogs on edge. Though his father had warned him to stay inside during his absence, the boy didn't want to take any risks with the sled dogs, so he grabbed a hatchet from beside the wood stove, pulled on a heavy coat and stepped out into the winter storm.

The snowstorm had built so that there was nothing for his pale eyes to cling to, just a vast blinding emptiness of sky and land, and no distinction between the two. He intended to turn towards the kennel where the loyal dogs yelped and whined, but instead, without really wanting to, the boy turned toward the seashore in the opposite direction. There was a strange song in the air, somehow audible through the howling wind, pulling his ear and luring him toward the frozen sea. He couldn't make it out; he wasn't sure what it was, but he found it captivating. The boy was strangely compelled to seek out its source.

Unable to stop himself, and despite his father's admonishments to always avoid the ice, he walked out onto the frozen inlet, across ice blushed pink and yellow by the sun and around blocks of turquoise ice as big as houses, their surface as smooth to the touch as sculpted marble. Ahead, there was a large crack in the ice through which black, frozen waters lapped. The boy was drawn to it even though somewhere in the recesses of his brain a warning screamed to stop, recognizing the danger that open, unsafe ice represented.

The boy's eyes widened as hag-like woman with a lumpy, scaled hide and tangled black hair rose from the water. He screamed and wanted to flee but found his legs were no longer under his control. They felt heavy and unresponsive, as if encased in thick ice. He stood rooted to the spot even as webbed hands with long, green nails reached out for him. Even as these powerful hands pulled him into the frigid water and dragged him into the dark depths of the ocean, still he could not move. He felt like he was plunging down a frigid well wrapped in a straightjacket. His world grew dark and cold. Death tapped him on the shoulder, and he embraced it as the last gasps of air escaped his lungs in a string of tiny air bubbles. And then, there was only blackness.

This helpless boy was yet another victim of the Qallupilluk, a sinister monster of the northern seas rightfully dreaded by the Inuit. Like every victim of this Arctic fiend, the boy's absence left an empty home and broken-hearted parents.

The Qallupilluk (sometimes spelled Qalupalik) are humanoid hags—for they are always female—with long hair, green skin and long fingernails. They reside in Arctic waters, either along frigid seashores or sometimes in bone-chillingly cold lakes and rivers. Qallupilluk prey on humans. Sometimes they use a humming sound to draw their prey, siren like, to open water and into their sodden grasp. Other times, they wait near gaps and weak points in the ice and listen for the footsteps of people above, tapping insistently on the ice like trapped seals, in the hopes of drawing the curious onto dangerous ground where they might break through and be drawn into the frigid waters. Sage Elders would patiently explain to youngsters that if the rapping wasn't a lurking Qallupilluk, then it might also be the sound of unsafe ice buckling or breaking. In either case, it wasn't safe and children hearing that telling noise should make for shore.

According to the legend, there are some warning signs when a Qallupilluk might be nearby. They reputedly smell of sulphur. They may also hum incessantly. And if the water begins to become wavy in only one confined area or steam begins to rise from its surface, a Qallupilluk might be hiding out of sight just beneath the surface. It's important to heed these signs; they may be the only warning you get before the aquatic hag springs her ambush, pouncing on you with a body dripping with icy water and with claws honed to a razor-sharp finish.

No one really knows why these creatures love to take children. It seems likely that they are resentful of the fact they are unable to reproduce and crave the company of little ones. As a result, they will snatch up any youngsters who are foolish enough to ignore their parents' warnings and wander off alone or too near the water. Once engulfed in the hag's long arms, victims are stashed away in the hood of the *amautik* (an Inuit parka) every Qallupilluk wears and then carried underwater where they are adopted as the monster's own offspring. There's an even more dire possibility. What if the sea hags just like the taste of plump, tender children and consider them a delicacy? In either case, a child unfortunate enough to be taken by a Qallupilluk is not seen again.

The Qallupilluk has become something of an Arctic boogeyman that Inuit parents and Elders use to reinforce among children the dangers of wandering off alone, venturing too near dangerous shorelines, and most especially, walking out onto unsafe ice. Indeed, the cautionary tale of the Qallupilluk is still being told in schools, books and even on film (as seen in the 2010 stop-motion animation short, *Qalupalik*, by Ame Papatsie, produced by the Inuit Broadcasting Corporation and National Film Board of Canada).

But these hags don't only prey on naughty children who don't heed their parents' advice. It's believed the Qallupilluk called adults to their deaths as well. Alone in frozen, leaking cabins for months on end, many days travel from any other human and worn down by the unending cold, dark and solitude, some trappers succumbed to madness or "The Arctic Calls." They would feel the irresistible urge to walk into the ocean and sink beneath the waves, or might fearfully whisper about feeling the presence of a phantom rising noiselessly from the bay, coming to drag them back down the shore and into the frozen depths. Was this the Qallupilluk at work, or merely creeping madness?

Qallupilluk is just a myth, though. Isn't it? Not everyone is convinced. With only five percent of the world's oceans explored, and with new marine species being discovered all the time, some believe this sinister sea hag may be among the oceans' undocumented creatures. Noted cryptozoologist and author Ken Gerhard was part of a team behind the 2015 television show *Missing in Alaska*. In Episode 8 of the one-season program, entitled "It Lurks Beneath the Ice," the team investigated the Qallupilluk, what they referred to as a vicious Arctic mermaid that attacks unsuspecting people. Naturally, they found no concrete proof, but Gerhard left the door open, if only a crack, for the possibility that something is behind the Qallupilluk myth.

So what are we supposed to make of these strange tales? Are they just fanciful tales told to children as they were tucked under their blankets at night, intended to frighten and keep them safe? Or do the stories indicate that something could be lurking unseen within the cold northern waters? Without doubt, the harsh, threatening and desolate Arctic landscape makes it easy to believe in monsters hiding just out of sight.

One thing is certain. It's never safe to venture onto uncertain ice.

# Chapter 11

# Shuswaggi

~

From the deepest of lakes with sunless and freezing bottoms to shallow bodies whose waters are warmed by the sun, from remote wilderness lakes rarely seen by humans to those frequented by cottagers and vacationers, dozens of lakes across Canada are said to be home to elusive monsters that appear but infrequently and then disappear so quickly and completely it seems as though they are one with the water. Many people claim to have seen one, and many more have heard tell of one, but do lake monsters really exist?

First Nations Peoples have no doubt that the beast they call Shuswaggi exists. Indeed, they know to fear and respect it. As early as the 19th century, they were warning European travellers of the snake-necked, crocodile-headed monstrosity that hunts within British Columbia's Shuswap Lake. Most

Europeans who heard the tales scoffed, but some knew that every Native story had a grain of truth to it. A few have even seen the dread beast up close, recording encounters with a creature that should not exist, a creature out of prehistory.

Shuswaggi is a dark thing that lurks at the bottom of Shuswap Lake, a body of water not far from Lake Okanagan, which has its own mystery beast. On rare days—typically early in the morning—Shuswaggi breaches the lake's surface to survey its domain. When it does, the silhouette of its long, winding neck and massive humped body appear as if out of myth, startling onlookers and reminding us that little is known of the dark recesses of this ancient lake.

Located in the Okanagan Valley in central BC, Shuswap Lake formed millions of years ago from retreating glaciers. The lake is extremely deep, in places descending to depths of more than 160 metres. It is also a vast lake, measuring 88 kilometres long with four long arms that make it difficult to survey.

The Native Peoples of the region reported that the beast was one to be wary of. Its name means "water bear," suggestive of its power and savagery. According to First Nation tales, this creature has preyed upon unwary people and animals alike, and would even overturn boats to throw passengers into the water, where they would be pulled below, one by one, until no one was left to scream in terror.

In the December 1990 issue of *Fate* magazine, Richard Medley of Philomath, Oregon, recounted an encounter with Shuswaggi—or, as it is popularly known today, the Lake Shuswap Monster—that took place three decades earlier.

In the summer of 1962, Medley was vacationing along the southern shores of the lake, enjoying the tranquility of its setting and the bounty of its fishing. At dawn on a clear August morning, just as the sun was rising above the mountains and the songbirds were stirring, Medley grabbed his rod and headed out on foot from the rustic cabin he was renting. His intent was to find a spot along the shore and spend the morning casting a line into the lake. He walked down to the railway tracks than run alongside the water and then followed them east. Medley trotted through a short tunnel that took the tracks through a rocky headland, eager to reach the spot just beyond where the shore drops off suddenly and plummets to great depths. It was here that he intended to find his morning idyll, fishing and lazing until the sun rose high overhead.

Things rarely work out as planned.

"As I emerged from the tunnel, however, I found that my intended fishing spot was taken by an empty houseboat that had apparently broken its mooring somewhere on the lake and had grounded on some rocks near the shore," Medley recounts. "While I stood looking at the houseboat, a movement in the lake approximately 300 feet [100 metres] offshore caught my eye. It was a glistening brown hump about two or three feet [60 centimetres or one metre] above the water level and about eight to ten feet [2.4 to 3 metres] long. In 1962 I had never heard of lake monsters, not even the Loch Ness phenomenon, and I stood totally perplexed as I watched the hump approach closer to shore."

An educated and clear-minded man, Medley tried to rationalize what he was witnessing, to find some mundane, plausible explanation. It was an exercise in futility.

"I first thought that it was a log; but then I noticed that it was creating a wake and realized that it was moving under its own power. Then I proceeded to consider beaver, otter, moose and bear, but immediately knew that the object was too large for the former and that the latter would not swim with their heads underwater. The hump continued moving toward shore until, within about 100 feet [30 metres], it suddenly turned and proceeded west around the headland and out of sight, leaving me baffled as to what I had just seen."

Medley never did find that morning idyll. Too startled by the experience and—he's not too ashamed to admit—a bit frightened, he instead chose to keep away from the lake for the remainder of his vacation. Before heading back to his home in the United States, Medley elected to spend a few days at nearby Okanagan Lake. There, he heard tales of that lake's famed monster, Ogopogo, and realized that what he had seen was very similar in description to the cryptid inhabiting Okanagan Lake's depths. Medley was forced to concede he had seen a lake monster, but it was only years later that he discovered others had reported run-ins with the same creature, that he was not alone in seeing a beast he learned was called Shuswaggi.

On June 3, 1984, Linda Griffiths was sailing Lake Shuswap with her two children and a young friend of theirs when she noticed a patch of water, about 100 metres from her, that suddenly began to churn violently. Linda had spent countless hours on the lake and had never seen anything like it, so naturally the churning caught her attention. Putting a pair of binoculars to her eyes, she zoomed in on the disturbance. And that's when she noticed seven large, greyish-brown humps coursing rapidly through the water in a straight line. It was immediately clear to her that this was one creature, not seven in tandem. The humps drew nearer, and when it crossed in front of her little sailboat Linda was able to get a better view of the creature. It was, she recalls, something resembling a snake, about 6 or 8 metres in length, but it swam with unusual vertical undulations that were unlike how water-faring snake species swim. Her children, aged 12 and 15, and their young friend, aged 13, all supported Linda's description.

Zach Brown had a similar experience three decades later while vacationing in the area. He was paddling his stand-up paddleboard across a lake that was as smooth as a pane of glass. It was late afternoon on a beautiful summer day, but there were few other people on the lake. As he dipped his paddle into the water, Zach happened to look down and noticed a dark shadow slide past beneath him. It was long and serpentine but darted through the water extremely fast, like a fish or otter. Suddenly, a trio of dark humps cut through the water, shattering the glasslike surface of the lake. The creature did a sudden 90-degree turn to pass directly in front of Brown at a distance of about 20 metres. A head rose from the water and turned toward the startled paddle-boarder, seemingly considering him with its unblinking black eyes. The jagged teeth that were revealed when it momentarily opened its mouth hinted at a primordial nature.

Brown was terrified and struggled to remain balanced atop a board that was now rocking violently as its owner shook with fright. The poor man was desperate to remain upright; to fall into the water put him at the mercy of this fearsome monster. Thankfully, after considering Brown for a few tense moments, the beast seemed to decide the man offered nothing of interest and slipped beneath the surface again. That was the last Brown saw of it, but needless to say, he raced for shore.

These reports are only a few of many that have emerged over the years from Lake Shuswap, and all the reports describe a similar monster. The colour varies from gray to black, but the physical description remains remarkably consistent: a creature that seems to exhibit the worst traits of a whale and snake, always measuring about 6 to 8 metres in length and always moving with the same undulations.

That the mystery creature moved with distinct lateral, rather than vertical undulations is an important observation. Although snakes don't move in such a manner, mammals can. This has helped cryptozoologists pinpoint a possible identity for Shuswaggi.

So what is this deep-dwelling lake monster that occasionally rises to the surface to terrorize people? Noted cryptozoologist Dr. Karl Shuker, something of an expert in the realm of aquatic monsters, believes he may know. Far from believing it's an aquatic snake of monstrous proportions, or even a classic Nessie-like plesiosaur, he firmly believes the Lake Shuswap Monster may in fact be a surviving zeuglodon.

Zeuglodons were prehistoric ancestors of modern whales that lived some 30 to 40 million years ago and were noted for having long, well-developed necks that could be raised out of the water. Although these primitive whales lived in the oceans of the prehistoric world and fossil evidence shows they could grow as much 20 metres in length, Shuker believes Shuswaggi might be a zeuglodon that adapted to freshwater and, as a result of the smaller body of water which it inhabits, grows to a more modest—though still colossal—8 metres in length. The zeuglodon seems to fit the Lake Shuswap Monster profile. It's even believed to have moved with the up-and-down undulations noted by so many Shuswaggi eyewitnesses.

If indeed the zeuglodon didn't become extinct 25 million years ago and still exists within the deep, lightless depths of Lake Shuswap, it's a good thing that stand-up paddle-boarder Zach Brown was able to maintain his balance and remain out of the water. The zeuglodon was a voracious predator with jaws that could exert 1600 kilograms of pressure, far greater, for example, than modern crocodiles. Little wonder that First Nations Peoples of the Okanagan Valley would fear such a monster.

While less well known than Ogopogo of nearby Lake Okanagan, Shuswaggi is every bit as mysterious...and perhaps even more frightening, if folklore and eyewitness accounts are to be believed.

Zoologists assure us that lake monsters like Shuswaggi cannot possibly be real, and scientists assert that they are nothing more than folklore and urban legend. Yet, Shuswaggi, like Ogopogo, the Loch Ness Monster and Champ, continues to be seen even as it continues to elude capture and identification.

Thus, the legend of Shuswaggi continues to thrive.

# Chapter 12

# Yellow Top

~

Bigfoot, or Sasquatch, needs no introduction. Large and powerful hominids, covered in coarse hair, standing more than 2 metres in height and weighing more than 135 kilograms, they instill both fear and curiosity. Bigfoot are virtually synonymous with the forested mountains of the Pacific Northwest, where the vast majority of sightings have occurred and where their legend has reached epic proportions.

But Sasquatch are not confined to the mountains of the west. Reports of a large, hairy, ape-like creature haunting the mining region near Cobalt, in northeastern Ontario, are numerous and stretch back to the earliest years of human habitation in the region. This elusive beast seems to be a subspecies of Sasquatch; the only apparent difference between the hairy man-ape of northern Ontario and those of the Pacific coast is the light-coloured hair that covers its head, neck and shoulders. It is from this distinctive coloration that the creature's nickname, Old Yellow Top, derives.

Northern Ontario's unique subspecies of Sasquatch emerged from the shroud of myth and folklore more than 100 years ago, in September 1906. The area around Cobalt was then a largely unsettled frontier, and the mining frenzy that would turn the community into the most productive silver-producing town in the British Empire was only in its infancy, so there were few humans in the imposing wilderness. Spurred on by dreams of overnight riches, prospectors pushed deeper into rugged forests that had rarely, if ever, been trod by European feet before.

One group of silver-seekers had pushed deep into the woods east of Cobalt, where they began building the headframe of the soon-to-be-famous Violet Mine, labouring feverishly to raise the structure so they could begin extracting ore from the ground. The ringing of the hammers must have disturbed something that lurked in the forest because an ape-like creature emerged from the forest to investigate the unusual sounds. Sniffing the air and shuffling nervously on bowed legs, the beast observed the work crew intently for long minutes, head tilted as it tried to make sense of these unfamiliar beings. The anxious workers were nearly paralyzed with fear. Every one of them was convinced that what they beheld was no bear, and so they gripped their tools tighter, afraid that the monstrosity would turn violent. They held their collective breaths, paralyzed with fear, praying that the beast would lose interest and shuffle back into the dark depths of the forest.

The creature continued to watch the workers for several long minutes until its shape blended in with the trees at the edge of the clearing once more, and it was gone. When at last the men completed the headframe and returned to civilization, they told their sensational story, and a news-starved media picked it up in papers that appeared across the English-speaking world. Bold headlines called the creature the Traverspine Gorilla or the Precambrian Shield Man.

More than a decade later, in July 1923, two prospectors, experienced woodsmen by the names of J.A. MacAuley and Lorne Wilson, were taking test samples of their mining claims northeast of the Wettlaufer Mine northeast of Cobalt when they saw what initially looked to be a bear feasting in a blueberry patch nearby. With courage that bordered on recklessness, Wilson threw a stone at the animal, hoping to frighten it off. Its response was immediate and terrifying.

The creature stood up to its full height on two legs, towering over both men. This was no bear, the prospectors realized with growing terror. The 2-metre tall man-beast bared its teeth and let out a roar of defiance. The sound was ear-piercing and dreadful, like nothing either man had ever heard before, a sound that melted courage and left these grown men shaking to their very cores. Driven by pure fear, they fled and didn't stop running until they reached the safety of town. Though they eventually regained their senses, the horrifying details of their encounter and the creature's startling appearance remained etched forever in their minds. What they had initially mistaken for a bear was in fact a humanoid in every way similar to the Sasquatch of the west, except for one important detail: "It's head was kind of yellow," remembered Lorne Wilson when interviewed for a newspaper story, "and the rest of it was black like a bear, all covered in hair."

MacAuley and Wilson returned to the wilderness afterwards—the lure of silver riches too strong to ignore—but they were never again so cavalier about its dangers. They knew, even if others doubted, that they had encountered something monstrous. Both men went to their graves convinced they had seen Old Yellow Top.

Another well-documented sighting took place in April 1946 near the hamlet of Gillies Depot. It was early morning when a woman and her young son began the long walk along the railway tracks into Cobalt to do the family's weekly shopping. As it was early spring, the woman was wary of stumbling across young bear cubs and their protective mothers, and so she jumped when a large shadow in the periphery of her vision moved toward the tracks. She swept her young son into her arms, using her slender body to shield him from any danger that might present itself. But what she saw shocked her beyond belief. This was no bear, nor a wolf or any other creature she was familiar with. The woman described it as more man than beast, walking on two legs like a man, and in her terrified mind, she knew this was the legendary Old Yellow Top featured in so many of the stories miners used to regale youngsters. The frightened woman held her son close, but they held no interest for the beast. It casually ambled across the tracks and disappeared into the woods on the other side, leaving the shaken onlookers to continue their journey. The *North Bay Nugget* for April 16, 1946, noted that, in that wake of this woman's terrifying ordeal, "a search party was formed to try and find 'Old Yellow-Top.'" The paper made no mention of what these men planned to do should they find the elusive beast, but the implication was clear: they intended to kill it.

The most famous—and controversial—encounter with Old Yellow Top occurred on an August night in 1970. The evening had begun normally enough. The sun had long since set, and the night was dark and still when 26 miners bound for a graveyard shift at the Cobalt Lode Mine clambered aboard a bus driven by Aimee Latreille. The bus lurched forward along eerily black rural roads, and soon many of the miners began dozing lightly on uncomfortable seats before their long shifts. As the sounds of snoring drifted toward him, Latreille expertly guided the bus along the road. It was a journey he had taken numerous times before, always without incident. This night, however, would be quite different.

Latreille was startled by a dark form that suddenly emerged from the forest to walk across the road in front of the bus. Reacting instinctively, he slammed on the brakes and swerved to avoid a collision. The bus hit the soft shoulder, and Latreille's eyes grew wide in panic as he lost control of the vehicle and it skidded towards a precipice that would drop them down a deep, rocky embankment. Finally, at the last possible moment, the brakes caught in the sand and the bus slid to a stop. Heart still pumping with the adrenaline of the moment, Latreille gazed over the bus' hood and saw only the blackness of empty space.

It's hard to say exactly what unnerved the driver more, his near brush with death or the nature of the creature he almost hit. "At first I thought it was a big bear," Latreille told reporters afterwards, "but then it turned to face the headlights, and I could see some light hair, almost down to the shoulders. It couldn't have been a bear. I have heard of this thing before but I never believed it. Now I am sure."

One of the miners at the front of the bus, a man named Larry Cormack, also caught a brief glimpse of the creature and supported Latreille's report that something had appeared momentarily in the headlights as it passed in front of the bus. He was less sure of what he saw; however, though admittedly he had a briefer view and from a less advantageous position

than the driver. "It looked like a bear, but it didn't walk like one. It was kind of half-stooped over," recounted Cormack. Then, as if trying to rationalize what he'd witnessed, he added, "Maybe it was a wounded bear, I don't know."

Sightings have continued. Lifetime Cobalt resident Bill McKnight passed away in 2014 but went to his grave swearing Yellow Top was very real. He had seen the beast one day near the Violet Mine, which you'll recall was the site of the first recorded encounter with Yellow Top back in September 1906. The monstrous biped was in a clearing and, upon sensing McKnight's presence, fled behind a large pile of rock and vanished from view. The experience had taken only a few short minutes but stayed with the startled man for a lifetime.

Similarly, John Crane, a recreational hunter who has an almost encyclopedic knowledge of wildlife developed over the course of years spent enjoying the great outdoors, is certain of Yellow Top's existence. He knows what he encountered a decade ago while exploring the woods near the former community of Kerr Lake, just east of Cobalt, was no bear or any other animal widely accepted to inhabit North America. "It was a hairy man-like creature, probably seven feet [2 metres] tall, just walking through the woods," he said. "At one point it scrambled up a steep slope covered in skree from the old mines without breaking a stride. You or I would have to pick our way up that slope but this thing did it no problem."

A species as large as Yellow Top would need a vast range in order to maintain a sustainable population, so it should come as little surprise that sightings extend well beyond Cobalt to include most of northeastern Ontario and into northwest Québec.

Ken Mercer is a truck driver who spends countless hours driving the lonely highways of northern Ontario. He thought he'd seen it all until late one winter night a decade or so ago. Mercer was driving along Highway 144 near the tiny town of Gogama. There were few vehicles on this lonely stretch of road and kilometres between buildings, leaving him driving in pitch blackness. He drove in silence, watching the darkened countryside slide by.

Suddenly, something ran across the road in front of his truck. As the truck's light washed over the creature, he caught a glimpse of two hairy legs and a towering shape he estimated to be at least 2.4 metres in height. Ken only caught it in his headlights for a few brief seconds, but the creature was bipedal with hair a little lighter than that of a moose. The creature took such large strides that it crossed the highway in only a few quick steps and then cleared with ease the high snow bank that shielded the road along its sides. It disappeared into the blackness of the night without so much as a pause, leaving Ken to digest what he'd seen. Not previously a believer in anything paranormal, he was now forced to admit the existence of Yellow Top.

Virginiatown is a small mining community that nestles close to the Québec border east of Kirkland Lake. It's here, in this distant corner of Ontario, that our final experience took place in 1997.

Two men were driving down a gravel road northeast of the village, heading for a diamond drill hole where they intended to collect spring water. It was late fall, well after the trees had become barren skeletons, and there had been a fresh snowfall that blanketed the rugged landscape in a sheet of white. The lack of vehicle tracks or footprints in the new-fallen snow told the two men that they were the only ones to use the remote road recently, and they almost certainly were the only human beings in the area.

"I had just finished filling up my water jug when I saw something walk in front of the van. The headlights were on, and whatever it was broke the beam of light as it walked by," one of the eyewitnesses writes. "I assumed it was my friend, so I called out asking where he was going. To my surprise he replied from behind me, about five feet [1.5 metres] back. I asked him if he had seen what I had seen, and he confirmed that he had."

Their curiosity aroused, the men temporarily put aside their water jugs and trudged through the snow and mud, past the van to where they had seen the shape pass by. They stared into the gloomy forests and saw nothing, even though it had taken less them less than a minute to reach the spot and the skeletal trees meant their range of vision extended dozens of metres from the road. Whatever they had seen was capable of covering great distances in a short period, and of doing it soundlessly.

Whatever it was, it wasn't a bear or moose. The large footprints in the snow were evidence of that. They were unrecognizable to the men, both of whom were experienced outdoorsmen, but clearly bipedal and humanoid. Their jaws dropped open; Bigfoot, a modern myth according to many, was real!

The stunning experience has been seared into their minds, remaining vibrant and shockingly fresh despite the passage of two decades. "To this day I can still see this thing walk by the headlights of my van," the eyewitness writes, "it looked like a silhouette, a black shadow so to speak."

And so the cycle continues. Those who witness Old Yellow Top are convinced they've seen a sub-species of Bigfoot unique to the forests of northern Ontario, while cynics put forward varied theories to debunk them. The creature has only been seen sporadically over the years, which is perhaps little wonder when one considers the remoteness and sheer expanse of the wilderness it calls home. But regardless of however infrequently Yellow Top is encountered, the mystery that surrounds it will always remain. After all, it's been more than 100 years since the first sighting, yet we're no closer to a definitive answer. And so the question remains: Do elusive man-apes slip through the forests in the Cobalt area? A century of gripping encounters suggests that perhaps they do.

# Chapter 13

# Crescent Lake Monster

~

Newfoundland is home to numerous icy lakes, carved from the mountainous terrain by ancient glaciers. One particularly cold, deep body of water—Crescent Lake, located near the small town of Robert's Arm in the remote western reaches of the island province—is home to an elusive monster known as Cressie.

As with many Canadian lake monster traditions, this one began centuries ago with the First Nations Peoples in the area. The Beothuk who inhabited Newfoundland shivered in fear at the beast that dwelt within the lake's icy waters and terrorized the region. Legends suggested the monster slumbered for decades before awakening to feed in a ravenous frenzy. Although the monster was elusive to the point of being practically invisible, it caused chaos whenever it shook off its sleep and rose to the surface. Boats were sunk, wildlife upon which the natives depended for food were slaughtered or scared away and some fisherfolk never returned home from a day on the water. To warn their children away from the dangerous lake, parents told them the monster would drag them under the water and eat them if they weren't careful. Perhaps understandably, the mer-beast was viewed as a demon and was called Woodun Haoot, which means "pond devil," or Haoot Tuweyee, "swimming devil."

The Beothuk gave Europeans similar warnings when they arrived in Newfoundland in the 17th and 18th centuries. Early on, most Europeans viewed tales of Woodun Haoot as local myths and scoffed at them. However, by the late 1800s, white settlers were also sharing their stories of seeing the terrifying lake monster. Probably the first recorded sighting of Woodun Haoot by a European occurred in the 1890s when a local woman named "Grandmother Anthony" spied a giant serpentine creature swimming in the lake while she was picking wild berries along the shore. Since then, there have been dozens of recorded sightings.

Woodun Haoot was the talk of the town after a memorable encounter from the 1950s. On the day in question, two local woodsmen on the shores of Crescent Lake noticed what they took to be an overturned rowboat just offshore. Concerned about the fate of the boat's occupants, the men raced down to the water's edge and climbed aboard their own boat. They never stopped to wonder why or how the upturned boat was drifting against the wind. As the woodsmen drew near the "overturned rowboat," they were shocked to discover it was actually a huge, black serpent that silently slipped beneath the water's surface. Though both men had lived their entire lives in Robert's Arm, neither had ever seen anything like this before, and they didn't mind admitting later that it terrified them so badly that they wasted no time in getting back to dry land.

Although periodic reports of the Woodun Haoot were made throughout the 20th century, it wasn't until the latter half of the century that the creature became a regular feature of the lake, and people started referring to it as Cressie. But a silly-sounding name playing off Scotland's Nessie didn't do much to lessen some Roberts Arm residents' fears about its lurking presence in their shimmering lake.

Cressie is described as being long, thin and dark. She does not appear to have any fins or mane, and her body has an oily sheen. Her movement in the water is typically described as "rolling" or "undulating," her elongated body producing humps as she swims. Reports suggest Cressie is between 4 and 6 metres long. Some naysayers have suggested that because judging size on water is especially difficult without proper cues, the creature may not approach these monstrous dimensions. Perhaps not, but she's certainly large enough to impress upon residents that something frightening inhabits Crescent Lake.

In fact, a number of locals have been hunted and haunted by the Crescent Lake monster in recent years.

In the early hours of a spring day in 1990, an eyewitness saw an unusual patch of churning water just offshore at the southern end of the lake. He watched as a slim, black shape rose momentarily from the disturbance. Seconds later, it slid beneath the water and was gone.

Then on July 9, 1991, a Robert's Arm resident named Fred Parsons saw something unusual in Crescent Lake. A retired schoolteacher and newspaper correspondent, Parsons was a reasoned and logical man who believed in fact rather than fantasy. While boating on the lake one day, he was

startled to see something large surface not far from his bob-
bing craft. It was like nothing he had ever seen before, dark
brown and almost viper-like, and more than 8 metres long. It
swam rapidly through the water in an undulating fashion for
a time and then dove below the surface, leaving the dumbfounded man alone with his disbelief. What the heck was that?
Parsons would ask himself that question many times over the
years, never coming up with a satisfactory answer.

Just a few months later, on September 5, at 4:30 PM, a resident of Robert's Arm named Pierce Ridout was driving his
pickup truck toward town when he noticed a disturbance on
the surface of Crescent Lake. For three minutes he watched
what resembled the bow wave of a small boat about 150 metres
offshore, even though there was no boat in sight. He continued
watching and was rewarded with a remarkable sight: a black,
5-metre-long shape propelling itself out of the water in a way
reminiscent of a whale. Ridout noted the creature was long
and black, and didn't seem to have a head or neck, nor a fin,
sail or flippers. The creature dove below the water's surface
again and did not reappear. Ridout had previously loudly ridi-
culed the idea of a monster in Crescent Lake but was forced to
re-evaluate his position after his experience.

Other encounters followed. In the summer of 2003, a local
woman named Vivian Short saw the monster, which she
described as serpentine with a fish-like head. Around the
same time Ada Rowsell, the town's clerk, told a CBC reporter
that Short wasn't alone in seeing Cressie around that period.
"I've had several reports of sightings—people sighting some
kind of a huge monster or sea serpent or some kind of a fish,"
she said. Then, in 2015, an angler named Lyle claims to have
been chased from the lake by Cressie. He says the creature
surfaced only a few short metres from his boat and glared at

him with black, soulless eyes. It then dove under the water and threw its body against the bottom of the boat. There was a second bang, and then another, as Cressie repeatedly battered the boat from below. Lyle's hair stood up on end as fear coursed through his body. He felt threatened. *No fish is worth this*, he reasoned and headed for shore as quickly as possible. Even as he rowed for shore, the creature continued to bang against the hull's bottom as if herding the man and ensuring he knew—in no uncertain terms—that he wasn't welcome on the lake.

Cressie has also been linked by some to an unusual phenomenon associated with Crescent Lake. During winter, Crescent Lake freezes into a thick, solid sheet of blue ice. Numerous fishermen trudge out onto the ice to dip a line into the frigid water. But once out there, these individuals frequently find mysterious holes in the ice. These holes are not perfectly cylindrical, as made by an auger, but rather ragged and irregular. These ruptures seem to have been made by something bursting up and out from below, leading some to hypothesize they are in fact breathing holes made by Cressie.

It's entirely possible that Cressie isn't merely confined to Crescent Lake. In the 1980s a bush pilot crashed his plane into a nearby lake, South Pond, and tragically drowned. The terrible duty of recovering the body from the deep fell to a pair of RCMP divers. While underwater, the officers were reportedly assaulted by one or more aggressive creatures, eels of extraordinary size, all gnashing teeth and thrashing tail, as thick as a man's thigh, which emerged suddenly from the gloom. The panicked divers desperately kicked their fins in a race to the surface, hoping to escape the vicious attack. Thankfully, whatever had attacked them made no effort to pursue the divers. Even once safely back in their boat, panting with fear and exertion, the officers felt strangely vulnerable. It took them a long time to calm their shaken nerves enough to get back in the water to complete their task. It's been asserted that the divers described something far more terrifying than massive, aggressive eels when they first surfaced but later changed their story out of fear of public ridicule.

The usual explanations are given by skeptics to explain away Cressie, including swamp gas, floating logs or bubbles of gasses produced by decomposing pulpwood littering the lake bottom. Naysayers point out that there has never been a carcass or even a photograph to provide some form of tangible proof of the creature's existence. Locals, however, are certain Cressie is a real animal. They may be right. Crescent Lake is connected to the Atlantic Ocean by Tommy's Arm Brook, so it's possible that *something* might have migrated from the ocean's depths to the inland lake.

One hypothesis is that Cressie is an abnormally large eel. Certainly, accounts given by eyewitnesses are reminiscent of an eel, and eels can grow quite sizable. The marine conger eel, for example, routinely reaches lengths of 2 to 3 metres, while the Pacific moray grows up to half a metre longer, or more. Science suggests there may in fact be much larger eel species somewhere in the dark recesses of the world's oceans. In the 1930s, Danish marine biologists discovered evidence of the possible existence of a 20-metre eel when they found a deep-sea eel larva measuring 2 metres in length, 25-times larger than normal eel larvae. It's therefore possible that one or more eels may have swam the 3 kilometres up Tommy's Arm Brook, taken residence in Crescent Lake and grown to fantastic lengths in the depths of the lake. This is actually entirely consistent with the behaviour of North American freshwater eels, which hatch at sea and make their way to freshwater systems as they mature, reaching maturity in lakes and ponds before returning to the sea as adults to spawn and die.

So why has no one seen huge eels migrating up Tommy's Arm Brook? Maybe they don't have to. Crescent Lake is more than 100 metres deep in places, putting its bottom below the low-tide level of Robert's Arm Harbour a kilometre away. Some locals have hypothesized that there may be a subterranean link between these two waterways and have cited the fact that some early lakeside residents occasionally complained of drawing brackish, salty drinking water from wells. Is there a layer of ocean water at the bottom of Crescent Lake? If so, Cressie need only migrate 100 metres to down to spawn, rather than brave the journey down Tommy's Arm Brook.

But there are those who point out aspects of the eyewitness testimonials that are inconsistent with eel physiology and behavioural norms. First, there is the matter of size. No eel on record has ever grown as large as the 7 to 13 metres length ascribed to Cressie. Then there is the fact that eyewitnesses invariably describe the creature swimming on the surface of the water and moving in an up-and-down fashion, both of which are completely wrong for an eel. Eels, in fact, are bottom-dwelling creatures and their locomotion, while wave-like, is side-to-side. Finally, most eels are nocturnal, whereas Cressie is frequently seen during the daytime.

Some who have studied Cressie lore over the years have come to the conclusion the "monster" is actually a very mundane animal, the northern river otter (*Lontra canadensis*). Here's how their reasoning works. The otter is dark in colour, swims both under the water and on the surface, and is diurnal in its activities. Multiple otters have been witnessed swimming in a line, one after the other, giving the illusion of a single large serpentine creature slithering with an undulating movement through the water. Even a single river otter can create a wake that will make it appear much longer than it actually is.

Still other doubters believe Cressie is simply a very old and very large sturgeon, an ancient fish called the coelacanth, thought to be extinct until the late 1930s, or even waterfowl or seals swimming in a row.

These theories are sound, particularly the convincing river otter theory. But while these undoubtedly work fine for people who have only spotted Cressie from a distance, where a number of factors can distort our perception, what of those who have seen her close up? Are we to believe these people have mistaken a relatively common, relatively small mammal (or worse, ducks or fish) for a giant serpent-like monster?

Theories like these don't hold much water with those who have reported Cressie sightings. They know what they saw. They know something large and aggressive lurks in the frigid depths of Crescent Lake. They just don't know what it is. Some, haunted by the experience, don't want to know.

# Chapter 14

# Devil Monkey

~

In the summer of 2006, Caitlyn had to go to out of town for business. She would be gone for a week, so she asked her mother to come and stay at her rural New Brunswick home with her two young daughters. Her mother agreed and Caitlyn left, unconcerned because she knew her children were in good hands.

After a few days, however, she noticed a change in her mother's voice during their nightly phone call. Finally, Caitlyn pressed her mother to share what was wrong. She expected perhaps to hear that her daughters weren't behaving, or perhaps one was ill or hurt herself while playing in the yard. Caitlyn couldn't have predicted what her mother would actually say.

"Early one morning, my mother was standing by the kitchen window drinking coffee when two deer ran past with their tails in the air, clearly afraid of something. My mom looked in the direction they had come from and saw something she can't explain. It had shaggy fur, a bushy tail like a coyote, big yellow eyes and a sort of bushy mane around its furry head. It stood on two legs and raised its head high, as if sniffing the air. Its nose was black and was at the end of a dog-like muzzle, and its arms were really long and hung loosely at its sides. She could distinctly see fingers on the hands. After a few seconds, the creature dropped back to four feet and raced off to the wood line, where it disappeared," Caitlyn writes.

"Now, you should know that my mother is a pragmatic farmwoman who has grown up in the area and is familiar with all of its wildlife," Caitlyn continues. "For her, things are as they are and she isn't given to imagination. She didn't mis-identify an animal like a raccoon, fox, coyote or bear. This wasn't like any animal she had ever seen. This was something unnatural, and it scared her."

This account is shocking, but it's hardly unique. Tales of similar creatures are widespread across Canada and the United States, and cryptozoologist Loren Coleman, who has been chronicling reports of this kind for almost 30 years, has dubbed the creatures Devil Monkeys.

To many observers, Devil Monkeys appear to be a kind of baboon. While accounts vary in some details, a "typical" Devil Monkey description is as follows. They are covered in short shaggy hair that ranges from red to brown to black. They have a barrel chest, powerful legs, long arms and a face described as being baboon- or doglike, with dark eyes and pointed ears. Footprints reveal a flat foot, thinner than that of a human of comparable size, measuring 30 centimetres long with three distinctive toes. Devil Monkeys can stand on their hind legs but move about on all four, leaning on their forelimbs. Movement is a shuffling run, leaping as do many forms of monkey. They are suspected of being omnivorous, subsisting mostly on vegetation but supplementing their diet with bird eggs, insects, rodents and other small mammals. They can be aggressive on occasion, and in some cases have attacked livestock (in 1973, for example, cryptozoologist Loren Coleman investigated a case in Albany, Kentucky, where Devil Monkeys were supposedly responsible for a number of livestock killings).

Though it occurred south of the border, in the foothills of the Appalachian Mountains, the following encounter provides one of the best, most comprehensive eyewitness accounts of a Devil Monkey sighting. Debbie Cross lives on a wooded ridge just west of the expansive wilderness of the Shawnee State Forest. Just after midnight on the night in question, Cross was roused from her spot in front of the television by the agitated barking of her dogs in the yard outside. Reluctantly, she pulled herself off the couch to investigate. As soon as she turned on the porch light, Cross saw the strangest creature she could ever imagine, standing a mere 10 metres from the house.

"It was about three to four feet [1 to 1.3 metres] tall and grey in color, and it had large, dark eyes and rounded ears extended above the head," she related to researchers Ron Schaffner and Kenny Young. "It had real long arms and a short tail. It made a gurgling sound. From the available light, the animal appeared to have hair or fur all over its body about one and a half inches [3.8 centimetres] long."

The creature locked eyes with Cross for a few seconds, and then began to retreat from the light. Cross was struck by the unusual manner in which the creature moved, walking on its hind legs while using the knuckles on its front limbs on the ground one at a time. Rather than move in a fluid walking motion, it "skipped," bounding rather than walking. When Cross' dogs gave chase, the creature effortlessly jumped over a barbed-wire fence and disappeared into the darkness of the Appalachian night. Cross heard a strange screeching sound, unlike any she had ever heard before, shortly thereafter.

The notion of there being an undiscovered species of monkey or ape in North America seems a bit outlandish on the surface. However, there is no denying the fact that these creatures have reportedly been encountered in numerous locales around North America. Sightings come from as far afield as Alaska in the north, New Brunswick in the east and Louisiana in the south.

One of the first reported sightings occurred in 1959 when a "monkeylike creature" rushed the car of the Boyd family as they drove down a rural road in Virginia. Their young daughter, Pauline, who was curled up in fear in the backseat, later recalled the terrifying ape-like attacker: "[It had] light, taffy colored hair, with a white blaze down its neck and underbelly…it stood on two, large well-muscled back legs and had shorter front legs or arms." The monster left a physical reminder of the assault in the form of three long scratch marks in the car's paint. Pauline also recalled another encounter that occurred just days later in the same region: "Two nurses from the Saltville area were driving home from work one morning and were attacked by an unknown creature who ripped the convertible top from their car." Although they were terrified, the nurses escaped unharmed.

A decade later, the Devil Monkey captured newspaper headlines in Canada, as well. In 1969, numerous people swore they saw a monkey-like beast, standing about one metre tall, lurking in the forests near Mamquam, British Columbia. In a province famous for its Sasquatch sightings, these accounts stood out for chronicling a creature completely against type. Had the witnesses claimed to have seen hairy 3-metre-tall hominids, these stories would hardly have stood out. Instead, they centered around ape-like beings less than half the size of Bigfoot.

Unlike Sasquatch, the creature these witnesses described was not a part of popular consciousness. This lent additional weight to the accounts and attracted the attention of mystery ape researchers Rene Dahinden and John Green, who spent considerable time researching the accounts. They came away convinced the eyewitnesses were truthful. What's particularly interesting, though, is that Dahinden and Green came away with casts of distinctive, three-toed feet.

Sightings of Devil Monkeys have continued in the years since, and with greater frequency. In 2001, for example, a creature described as a "giant black monkey" was seen nine different times over the course of two weeks in rural New Hampshire. In fact, Devil Monkey sightings have become so widespread that the Animal Planet television show *Lost Tapes* dedicated a 2010 episode to the phenomenon.

Native American folklore is replete with creatures that could well refer to the Devil Monkey. In the United States, for example, Choctaw legend tells of the Nalusa Falaya, meaning "long evil being," thin, black, furred humanoid beings with beady eyes and long pointy ears. While Nalusa Falaya were said to stalk their victims by sliding on their stomachs like a snake, cryptozoologists believe this was merely allegory for the stealthy manner in which they could creep up upon you.

Here in Canada, we have a range of legendary creatures that may reflect various interpretations of the Devil Monkey. The Armouchiquois, for example, is described as a short, shaggy humanoid with long, skeletal limbs that lives in Ontario's forests. It can run fast and leap great distances. The Picquenyan and Agropelter were similarly described short, hairy beings standing about one metre with long, spindly legs. The latter were considered the bane of lumberjacks. Agropelters pelted humans with tree branches and were even believed to kill humans, dragging their corpses into the trees and stuffing them into hollow tree trunks. There were many more names for what was essentially the same creature, all of them eerily similar in description to the creature we now refer to as the Devil Monkey.

So, let's assume Devil Monkeys are real and not the stuff of legend and fantasy. What might they be? Is there an explanation for what so many people have been witnessing across North America, coast to coast, for hundreds of years? Clearly the suggestion put forward by doubters that Devil Monkeys are baboons that have escaped from a circus or zoo isn't plausible; reports are too widespread and go back too many years for that to be possible. But what if these doubters are inadvertently touching on something? What if the Devil Monkey is in fact a prehistoric, believed-to-be-extinct cousin of the modern baboon? A number of cryptozoologists—Bernard Heuvelmans, Mark Hall and Loren Coleman among them—believe this is a distinct possibility.

Those who subscribe to the prehistoric baboon theory point to fossil finds of a giant baboon, *Theropithecus oswaldi* (formerly *Simopethicus*), which was twice as big as *Theropithecus gelada*, the gelada baboon of Ethiopia. *Theropithecus oswaldi* was a very successful, adaptive and widespread species. While the modern-day gelada baboon is limited to the highlands of Ethiopia in northeast Africa, its Pleistocene ancestor ranged across most of the continent, with fossils being found in Algeria, Kenya, Morocco, Tanzania and South Africa. Evidence shows that the primate crossed the land bridge at Gibraltar and entered Spain. There have even been controversial findings suggesting *Theropithecus* spread as far as India.

*Theropithecus oswaldi* would bear some similarity to accounts of Devil Monkeys. Its size, about 130 centimetres tall and 100 kilograms, is consistent. So too are the physical characteristics.

Some other researchers suggest there is a primate closer to home than *Theropithecus oswaldi* that may be behind the Devil Monkey phenomenon in North America. They point their collective finger to Brazil, where fossil remains of a giant howler monkey have been discovered. Dubbed *Protopithecus*, this new specimen is estimated to have had a body mass of roughly 25 kilograms, and it measured about 115 centimetres without its tail—more than twice the size of the largest living monkey in Brazil, the endangered muriquis. Indeed, anthropologists and folklorists have concluded that this prehistoric monkey is likely the source of the legendary Caypore, a large, ape-like creature said to lurk within the impenetrable interior of the Brazilian rainforest. They suggest this legendary creature could have a basis in fact, if it represents sightings that were passed down orally through many generations.

Is it possible that *Protopithecus* was far more widespread than we previously thought, and that the Caypore migrated north through Central America into the United States and Canada where it has become known as the Devil Monkey?

Doubters of both *Protopithecus* and *Theropithecus* will say North America is not supposed to have any native apes and that to believe a species could survive 650,000 years without leaving a fossil record or being positively identified by modern science is pushing credulity. Proponents, on the other hand, will say that until very recently we didn't even know *Protopithecus* existed or that *Theropithecus* lived beyond the continent of Africa, suggesting new discoveries are being made every day.

Some might argue that speculation into the matter of Devil Monkeys seems like utter fantasy. But even though there is no evidence that *Protopithecus* or *Theropithecus* ever managed to reach North America before they presumably became extinct, can one completely discount the possibility of a primate migrating to Canada and the United States at some point? And if indeed they did migrate to North America, might they continue to live?

What do you think?

# Chapter 15

# Lake Nipissing Monster

~

Ontario's Lake Nipissing is distinctive in a number of ways. With a surface area of 873 square kilometres, it is the third-largest lake in the province excluding the Great Lakes. Lake Nipissing is also unusually shallow for such a large lake, with an average depth of only 4.5 metres. This shallowness makes the lake difficult to navigate, as there are many sandbars along its shoreline, but it is also a fisherman's paradise with more than 40 species at ideal angling depth.

Lake Nipissing is also unique for historical reasons. Located between the Ottawa River and Georgian Bay, it formed a link in a maritime highway between Montréal and the continent's interior that was used for centuries by French explorers and fur traders. Étienne Brûlé, the famed explorer and fur trader, was the first European to see the lake when he passed through in 1610.

There's a final distinction, one that usually only comes to light while people are sitting around a crackling fire on a cool evening, sharing tales that become more outlandish as the night wears on. Lake Nipissing, if you believe these late-night storytellers, is home to an aquatic beast that defies easy categorization.

It is a common fallacy to believe sightings of lake monsters began when the Loch Ness Monster grabbed headlines with the now-famous grainy image of a long-necked reptile gliding through the waters of the Scottish lake. The press had a field day a few years ago when it came to light that this photo might have been a hoax. However, mysterious and unidentified creatures—monsters—have been seen the world over for centuries. Sightings of something in the waters of Lake Nipissing predate the famed Nessie photo by decades, for example.

Most witnesses describe a large creature—perhaps as much as 5 metres long—serpentine in appearance, sometimes displaying "undulating humps" and a neck that occasionally rises out of the water. If true, then this definition effectively rules out any mundane animal—beaver, otter, fish, swimming moose or bear—as being the guilty party.

Like its Scottish cousin, Nessie of Loch Ness, the Lake Nipissing monster has a long history of sightings. We may never know for sure how far back into history accounts go, but we can say for sure that the Indigenous Peoples who lived in the region knew that the waters of the lake were home to something monstrous and terrifying.

One notable encounter involved a young girl back in the latter half of the 19th century. Together with her parents and

siblings, she had travelled north along the Nipissing Coloni-
zation Road linking Lake Rosseau with Lake Nipissing. The
family was settling what was still largely a frontier region and
were filled with excitement at the prospects for the future
and fear of the unknowns to come. Their fears were seemingly
realized when the wagon rattled along a length of shoreline
road. In the water about 80 metres distant was a large, dark
green creature that had a horse-like head atop a long neck.
The girl's mother told her and her siblings to lie down in
the back of the wagon and then pulled a tarp over them. The
father, meanwhile, urged their weary horses on as fast as they
could pull the wagon over the rutted road.

Jumping forward more than a century, there is the case of
vacationer JG Tetch. An avid fisherman, he was staying at
a lakeside cottage resort catering largely to anglers. It was
early autumn, and the morning was crisp and cool. The sun
was still low on the horizon, and a chilled breeze was blowing
across the placid surface of Lake Nipissing. Tetch had no
sooner climbed into the 4-metre aluminum boat and started
the outboard motor when he saw a black streak break the surface of the water about 30 metres off the dock. It was just
a momentary glance as the object disappeared seconds later,
and at first Tetch didn't think too much of it. An otter or beaver, he reasoned, maybe even fish. Certainly he didn't antici-
pate it was anything unusual.

He would be proven wrong. Perhaps an hour later, Tetch
was about 2 kilometres away from the resort and was happily
casting his line. There was a tug on his fishing line, and Tetch
began reeling in what he could tell by the fight was a sizable
catch. As he drew in the line, he caught a glimpse of a pike
putting up a valiant struggle. Then, Tetch saw a black shape
streaking past just below the surface, a large shadow he was

stunned to see was as long as the boat in which he sat. The creature aimed directly for the pike and then, seconds later, Tetch's line went slack as the pike no longer fought against it. When the angler finished reeling in the line, he could see why the fish had suddenly ceased struggling. There was nothing left of it, save for bulging eyes and gaping mouth of a severed head. The rest of its body had been violently ripped away.

Whatever the animal was that had snatched his morning catch, it was like nothing he had ever seen before. Tetch understandably felt somewhat vulnerable sitting in a thin-hulled aluminum boat with a hungry predator as large as that watercraft hunting nearby.

From scattered sightings over the last 125 years or so, we can assume the Lake Nipissing Monster has a large, horse-like head atop a long neck, is darkly coloured (accounts range from black to brown to dark green) and appears reptilian. The image of a plesiosaur, like the Nessie of popular imagination, is what immediately jumps to mind. Perhaps because of the shallowness of the lake, the Lake Nipissing Monster is described as smaller than most lake monsters in Canada at perhaps only 3 to 4 metres in length.

Marie Mercer recalls hearing her uncle recount an unusual experience he had on the waters of Lake Nipissing with an anomalous creature. Sadly, he has since passed so we can't hear the story first-hand, but the story stands out vividly in Marie's mind, and she agreed to share it with me for this book.

"My uncle, an avid fisherman, maintained for years that, on two occasions when he was out on his boat fishing in a favourite spot on Callander Bay [in south-eastern Lake Nipissing], he saw something with a head at least the size of a cow's head break the water not far from his boat. The creature continued to swim with its head up out of the water for a short distance before submerging again. On one of the outings, my uncle claimed to have been with a fellow fisherman, who saw the creature as well," she says. He wasn't weaving a tall tale, Marie asserts. While not afraid, he was genuinely unsettled by the experience. "I can tell you that he truly believed he saw something extraordinary when sharing his story with us for the first time some 35 years ago and again retelling it 10 years later."

Sadly, he didn't share more details, and at the time, Marie didn't think to push for them. She regrets that now. What is certain, however, is that as an avid sportsman who spent countless hours looking out onto the bay from his lakeside home, he was unlikely to misidentify a mundane aquatic animal, such as beaver, otter or muskrat.

It's interesting to note that Lake Nipissing is of considerable size, one in which a colony of predominantly underwater-based creatures could survive and thrive. At the same time, because Lake Nipissing is connected to Georgian Bay and Lake Huron via the French River, it has been hypothesized that the monsters said to be haunting these bodies of water represent the same species. Certainly, they bear striking similarities.

A creature similar to the Lake Nipissing Monster has been seen in nearby Trout Lake, raising the possibility it is in fact the same species. "There have been reports of large swells of water, shadows, figures of various proportions and sizes—much like the Loch Ness Monster," noted local historian and author Wilston Steer. "Trout Lake is a cold, deep lake. Its origins are linked to the last ice age of three thousand to five thousand years ago. It is almost 'bottomless.' Local sightings have included monstrous muskie, crocodile/alligator-like creatures and serpent-like creatures."

The Trout Lake Monster has even been blamed for the tragic disappearance of Margaret and Allen Campbell back in 1956. The couple simply vanished from their cottage. The family car stood in the driveway and remains of lunch were found on the stove. But there was absolutely no sign of the couple, nor their dog or their fiberglass boat. Police dragged the lake and scoured the shoreline, but no remains were ever found. Most would suggest the couple were murdered or drowned in the lake, but at least one researcher has suggested the Campbell's boat might have been overturned by the elusive monster rumoured to lurk within the lake and that, in a ravenous frenzy, it devoured the couple and their dog.

Thankfully, nothing so terrifying has ever been linked to the beast living in the depths of Lake Nipissing. True, Indigenous Peoples believed the Manitou Islands were haunted and quite possibly shrouded in evil, and avoided the area as a result, but of the monster itself there are no such horror stories.

There are undoubtedly other sightings of the Lake Nipissing Monster beyond those chronicled above that have yet come to light. In all likelihood, some sightings of such alleged creatures are due to mistaken identity. But there are those reports that simply cannot be dismissed in such a down-to-earth fashion, leaving us to draw the conclusion that Lake Nipissing may indeed be the lair of monstrous serpents of the deep.

As to what these monsters may be, the answers still elude us.

# Chapter 16

# Partridge Creek Monster

~

Canada's Arctic is undoubtedly the last place anyone might expect to meet a dinosaur. It is, after all, frigidly cold and remarkably inhospitable, a place only the hardiest of animals can endure. Surely, cold-blooded dinosaurs would be unable to survive in such a harsh landscape. Yet an account has emerged that suggests primeval reptiles have somehow adapted to Canada's tundra.

The so-called Partridge Creek Monster is one of the most unusual to emerge from the shadowy recesses of Canadian cryptozoology.

A bipedal dinosaur with a mouth filled with sharp teeth, short arms that end in vicious claws and a hide covered with shaggy fur, mercilessly hunting prey in the frozen wilderness of the Canadian north? Impossible, you say? That's exactly what readers a century ago thought. Yet it was recorded as fact.

The extraordinary tale of the Partridge Creek Monster stole the headlines of the April 15, 1908, edition of the French magazine *Je Sais Tout* ("I Know All"). The feature story, which left readers breathless and amazed, recounted the experience of an eyewitness named Georges Dupuy. It was written as fact, without the tongue-in-cheek tone of many monster accounts in newspapers of the period.

According to Dupuy, a supposed "world traveler," the adventure had begun one day five years earlier, in 1903, when James Lewis Buttler, a wealthy banker from San Francisco, and local gold prospector Tom Leemore were hunting moose in a marshy landscape near Yukon's Clear Creek, about 80 kilometres east of Dawson City. The two hunters spotted three large moose and began stalking them, slowly approaching to within rifle range.

Suddenly, one of the moose jerked its head, fully alert. It had clearly sensed something nearby that it considered a threat. Another moose then raised its head and began testing the air with its nostrils. It must have smelled something unnerving, because it emitted a loud bellow of alarm that sent all three moose fleeing southwards.

At first Buttler and Leemore were disappointed. The moose had fled before they had a chance to fire even a single shot. Then they were perplexed. They had been approaching silently from downwind, meaning the dim-sighted moose shouldn't have detected them. What then had caused three massive moose—each standing 2 metres at the shoulder and weighing more than 450 kilograms, with massive racks tailor-made for goring potential predators—to flee in abject terror?

The puzzle only grew more perplexing when Buttler and Leemore reached the spot where the moose had been grazing before their flight. In the snow was the clear impression of a massive body belonging to some unidentifiable beast of monstrous proportions. The beast's belly had ploughed a furrow estimated to be 10 metres long, 4 metres feet wide and 60 centimetres deep into the riverbed's swampy mud. Trailing behind was the impression of a tail measuring 3 metres in diameter. Even more terrifying than the obvious monstrously proportioned body that had left this impression were the gigantic footprints found alongside. They measured almost one metre across and 1.5 metres in length, with the distinctive imprint of razor-sharp talons measuring 30 centimetres long

Neither man had ever seen anything like these tracks before and couldn't imagine what manner of beast could possibly have left them. The tracks suggested something far larger—and far more horrifying—than any of North America's known wildlife. Their curiosity aroused, Buttler and Leemore put aside common sense and began following the tracks, hoping to catch a glimpse of, or perhaps even kill, the mysterious beast. The trail led several miles to a gulch known as Partridge Creek, where the tracks abruptly came to an end. The only explanation was that the animal had either taken flight—surely impossible in light of its massive dimensions—or else, as improbable as it may seem, had somehow leapt directly up into the gulch's cliffs. Since Buttler and Leemore had no means of climbing the cliffs, their monster hunt had drawn to a close.

The pair made their way by canoe along the McQuesten River to the nearby outpost of Armstrong Creek, a First Nations' village where Buttler had earlier arranged to meet Dupuy to take him hunting. Buttler and Leemore shared their experience of the anomalous tracks with Dupuy and a local Jesuit priest, Reverend Father Pierre Lavagneux, both of whom were understandably quite skeptical. The story sounded like pure fantasy. But Leemore and Buttler were insistent and offered to guide Dupuy and Father Lavagneux back to Partridge Creek to see the tracks for themselves, and perhaps even find the monster itself. Only then, they reasoned, with additional eyewitnesses, could they be vindicated and their story lent an air of authenticity.

By this time, the tracks had largely washed away. Nevertheless the party, accompanied by a number of Indigenous hunters, spent the better part of a day searching the area for any signs of a monstrous beast preying on moose and other fauna in the area. By nightfall, the group was weary and dejected. Their search had come up empty, just as the skeptical Dupuy and Father Lavagneux had expected it would.

The party set up camp. It wasn't long into the evening before they heard a spine-chilling roar. The startled hunters reached for their rifles, and one of them pointed with a shaking hand to the opposite side of the ravine. A monster, measuring 15 metres long and estimated by Buttler to weigh about 40 tons, was climbing up the side of the ravine.

Seemingly unaware or unconcerned with the terrified onlookers on the other side of the ravine, the monster continued to climb upwards. At one point it paused for 10 minutes or so, at a distance of about 200 metres, giving the party an opportunity to get a better look at the monster they had been hunting. Its hide was caked with mud and had bristly-hair, like that of a wild boar. A rhino-like horn protruded from the end of the creature's snout, and its ravenous maw was filled with razor-sharp teeth. It had clearly only recently fed, as tendrils of blood and saliva trailed from its mouth.

Some of the party stood frozen with terror, paralyzed by the terrifying reality of what they were seeing and the deadly threat it represented. Others cowered behind trees and rocks. A few brave souls brought their rifles to their shoulders, prepared to defend themselves should the monster attack.

Thankfully, the creature seemed unaware or uninterested in their presence. Instead, it suddenly reared up onto its massive hind legs, gave another ear-splitting roar that caused hair to stand on end and then leapt out of sight. And that was fine with the party. They had lost all appetite for hunting the beast and wanted nothing more than to leave it, and the terrifying memory of seeing it up close, behind forever. After a restless night in which no one slept out of fear of the creature's return, the men hurriedly packed up camp and began the journey back to Armstrong Creek.

Dupuy alone had an interest in continuing the hunt. He petitioned the territorial officials at Dawson City to supply him with a large-scale hunting party with 50 heavily armed men, but his request was declined. When this failed he returned home to France.

The story doesn't end there, however. In January 1908, Dupuy received a letter from Father Lavagneux, dated from the previous Christmas. What he read stunned him. According to the priest, the monster had been seen again. This time, it was seen racing along a frozen river with the carcass of a caribou dangling from its jaws. Tracks identical to those found back in 1903 were clearly visible in the snow and deep mud. Lavagneux and a party of First Nations men followed the trail for a while, but eventually fresh snowfall covered the tracks. Once again, the beast had eluded them.

As to what the monster was, no one knew for certain, though Father Lavagneux had an opinion. A supposedly

learned man, the priest was convinced the creature was a ceratosaurus (*Ceratosaurus nasicornis*), a large flesh-eating bipedal
dinosaur that was an evolutionary ancestor of the later, larger
Tyrannosaurus rex. Its most distinguishable feature was—
you guessed it—a large horn near the tip of its upper jaw, just
like that of the Partridge Creek Monster.

Father Lavagneux was no paleontologist, so he could be
excused for not appreciating how unlikely his claim was. Not
only would the survival of a ceratosaurus into the 20th century fly in the face of all we know of evolution and the devel-
opment of life upon our planet, but it also should be biologically
impossible for a reptile to survive, let alone thrive for millennia, in the cold of Canada's Yukon.

Not so fast! New research has indicated that dinosaurs
were able to survive much colder temperatures than previously thought. Paleontologists from the Royal Belgian Institute of Natural Sciences have unearthed a rich variety of

dinosaur bones, including ceratosaurus and duck-billed dinosaurs, in the far northern reaches of Russia. At the time these dinosaurs existed, average temperatures there would have been around 10°C. The scientists have also found eggshells alongside the Arctic dinosaur remains, providing the first proof that dinosaurs were able to reproduce in colder conditions. These findings suggest that dinosaurs were not confined to tropical zones as previously imagined and could in fact have adapted to colder climates. Professor Pascal Godefroit, who led the research on the polar dinosaurs, noted "there is no way of knowing for sure, but dinosaurs were probably warm-blooded just like modern birds, which are the direct descendants of dinosaurs...the dinosaurs were incredibly diverse in polar regions—as diverse as they were in tropical regions."

In other words, it is in the realm of biological possibility for a dinosaur to survive in Arctic conditions. But a century ago dinosaurs were assumed to be cold-blooded, like snakes and lizards, which cannot survive in cold climes. This leads to two possibilities: Either Dupuy and the others were making up a tall tale and simply guess correctly when they decided to transplant a dinosaur to the Yukon, or else they really did see what they claimed to have seen.

And what of the description of the Partridge Creek Monster having boar-like fur? Doesn't that outlandish statement cast doubt on the entire episode? It might, though it should be noted that scientists have proven that many dinosaurs, perhaps all, had some feather plumage. Even the mighty Tyrannosaurus rex is believed to have had feathers running down its back. From a distance, and matted with mud, feathers might look like fur. Again, there is no reason for people of a century past to think dinosaurs had any sort of body covering, be it hair or feathers; the science of the day assumed dinosaurs were completely covered in scales or thick, leathery hide. Furthermore, would it be possible for a dinosaur, over the course of millions of years, to have developed shaggy fur in order to adapt to Arctic conditions?

Paleontologists would undoubtedly rub their hands together in abject glee at the opportunity to debunk any notion that the Partridge Creek Monster was real, citing a host of sound scientific facts such as the unlikelihood of the creature surviving whatever global calamity caused the extinction of the dinosaur; the fact that bipedal dinosaurs did not drag their tails on the ground but rather held them horizontal to the ground; the unlikelihood that anything as large as a ceratosaurus could go unnoticed by modern humans and be completely absent in the oral lore of First Nations Peoples; and so on and so on.

Nothing has been heard of the Partridge Creek Monster since. Yet, despite the weight of scientific evidence, and perhaps even common sense, some cryptozoologists are convinced the story Dupuy related for *Je Sais Tout* has some bearing in fact.

What do you think?

# Chapter 17

# Dwarves

~

Before European contact, the North American continent possessed a number of civilizations with extremely advanced social sophistication and cultural organization. By the second millennium CE, the Cahokia on the Mississippi, the Mound Builders in the Ohio valley and the Southeast, and the Anasazi in the Southwest had all created thriving communities, vibrant cultures and vast trade networks. We know of these people because of the remarkable remains they left behind.

But were there other people who existed alongside these cultures, people who remain undocumented because of lack of physical remains and their diminutive size? Did a race of dwarves, or "proto-pygmies" as researcher Ivan Sanderson labeled them, exist in the shadows of the North American landscape?

The notion of an undiscovered race of dwarves seems a bit outlandish on the surface. However, there is no denying the fact that these beings have been a part of lore and tradition in cultures the globe over. Indeed, there has even been physical proof of their existence: In 2003, a joint Australian-Indonesian team of archeologists discovered the remains of nine 1-metre-tall hominids on Flores Island. According to anthropologists that have studied these remains, these hominids—dubbed *Homo floresiensis*, or Flores Man, but nicknamed "hobbits"—represent a pygmy-sized side branch of human evolution that existed until as recently as 13,000 years ago. Though their brain mass was significantly less than that of modern humans, these beings demonstrated significant intelligence in using stone tools, painting pictograms, utilizing fire and hunting communally. The discovery of *H. floresiensis* has lent some credence to the Sumatran myth of the Orang Pendek ("Little Man"), a type of dwarf previously thought to be nothing more than an Indonesian legend.

Many Indigenous Peoples of North America similarly have tales involving mysterious and secretive people of diminutive stature. Some nurse spite and bitterness for humanity in the seclusion of dark forests. Others are cruel as the wickedest devil, luring people to their doom. Still more take special pleasure in tormenting humans by stealing babies, spoiling crops and playing mischievous tricks. A few even might lend aid, generally for some minor gift. The dwarves of North American Indigenous Peoples' lore are widely varied in form and nature. The following are but six types of dwarves that lurked on the fringes of civilization, though many more were known to exist (indeed, most First Nations cultures had stories of small people).

DWARVES

**Apci'lnic:** Standing only knee high, Apci'lnic stalk the mountains and forests of Labrador. These oft-cursed beings spread misfortune, and they delight in seeing others come to harm. In particular, they delight in stealing human babies and taking them back to the bottomless caverns they call home.

**Ardnainig:** A race of child-sized hairy men, they range in size from a relatively towering 1.5 metres down to barely more than 75 centimetres. The Ardnainig linger in the world's dark and unseen reaches and particularly favour the Arctic tundra and ice floes. Inuit were fearful of them, owing to the maniacal grimace that perpetually etched their weathered faces. The Ardnainig had normal-sized wives, sometimes stolen from human communities, who carried the Ardnainig on their backs.

**Jogah:** The Iroquois believed in a broad family of nature spirits, called Jogah, which took the form of dwarves. The Gahonga dwelled under rock mounds, in caves or beneath the waters of rivers. Gandayah, also known as "stone throwers" for their penchant for mischievously throwing rocks at people, were responsible for maintaining the fertility of the earth. They lived within large rocks. The Ohdows lived within the darkest tunnels of the underworld and rarely ventured into the sunlight.

**Megamawesu:** The little people of New Brunswick, the average Megamawesu stand one metre tall. According to the Mi'kmaq, these mean-spirited beings take disproportionate amounts of pleasure from the accidents and missteps of humans, many of which they manufacture through magic, traps and tricks. Megamawesu live in caves and occasionally venture forth at night to dance under the moon, cast their magic and find victims upon which to inflict their sick senses of humour. You can escape from a Megamawesu by crossing a creek because they hate getting their feet wet.

**Picquenyans:** When explorer Jacques Cartier returned to France from Canada, he thought he brought with him not only knowledge of a new land but also the existence of a new race. Chief Donnaconna, who had befriended Cartier, told him of the existence of a race of short men, known as Picquenyans that inhabited modern-day Québec. They were reclusive and few in number, which explained why Cartier never encountered them himself.

**Yunwi Djunsti:** Yunwi Djunsti were largely indistinguishable from First Nations people, save for the fact they stood barely 75 centimetres tall. These tiny beings had long black hair that trailed down their backs to drag upon the ground. They wore white clothes, which gave them an ethereal appearance when they would frolic in the woods under the pale light of the moon. Mischievous beings, they could become invisible to the naked eye on a whim and would play pranks or steal from humans.

Indigenous Peoples south of the border have their own legends about races of little people. The Crow have myths referring to *Nirumbee*, ferocious and powerfully built dwarves with sharp teeth and potbellies, that reside below the Pryor Mountains. The Nez Perce of Idaho speak of the *Itse-ya-ha*, which have been a part of their culture so long they are depicted in ancient pictographs. To the Arapaho, dwarves are known as *Hecesiiteihii*. And so on. The point being, tales of small people that lived alongside humans reach across the entire continent.

These dwarves, or "proto-pygmies," generally shared some characteristics. They were much smaller than most humans and never stood more then 1.25 metres in height but often much less. They were usually slender, covered in black or red fur, and had long, mane-like hair on their heads. Their faces were humanlike but with primitive, slightly ape-like features.

But has physical evidence of dwarves ever been discovered? If one believes an article in the *Toronto News* of January 2, 1891 (and later reprinted in the *San Francisco Chronicle*), the answer is a resounding yes. According to the feature, entitled "Unearthed Remains of a Dwarf Race," labourers in British Columbia at place called Macauley's Point stumbled upon ancient human remains in small burial mounds. The discovery was one of pure accident.

"A workman clearing away what he thought was a natural rise in the ground touched a hard metallic substance with his pick," noted the article. "On digging further, the object came to view. It was an iron weapon shaped like a harpoon, only much shorter and stouter. Curious characters were etched on it, and their lines had survived through centuries."

Naturally quite excited by the find, the worker and some companions dug deeper into the hillock. The article reports what they found:

> One of the mounds was excavated and a flat stone was exposed. It had been designed as a door to a sepulchre, for on being raised a grave, walled on all sides by tightly cemented stones, was seen. In it was a dwarfed body doubled up in a sitting position, a custom followed by the ancient Indian tribes along the entire Pacific coast. The body, though small, was that of an adult dwarf. Several other graves were opened and the occupants of all of them were in similar anatomical construction and size. In many of the graves roughhewn utensils, evidently used for cooking, were found, together with arrowheads known to have been used by coast tribes extinct for centuries.

Perhaps these mounds contained the earthly remains of Atnan, a race of dwarves referred to by First Nations in British Columbia. (Some people have even claimed to have seen the Atnan into modern times, at places as diverse as Francois Lake, Eutak Lake and Stuart Lake, suggesting these little beings are still with us, if in limited numbers.)

Sadly, we have no record of what befell these remains, though the article does mention that they caused "great excitement" in the area. We don't even know for certain how much of this story is real, but it represents a tantalizing possibility that a race of diminutive "proto-pygmies" may have existed in North America alongside the ancestors of our First Nations, or perhaps even in small pockets into relative recent history.

This wasn't even the first time that graves of dwarves had been uncovered in Canada. Captain Luke Foxe, a British explorer intent on finding the famed Northwest Passage between the Atlantic and Pacific oceans, discovered his own three centuries earlier. During his fruitless 1631 expedition, Foxe's crew found a number of graves containing people measuring less than 1.25 metres tall. According to Inuit with whom Foxe spoke, these graves belonged to a race of elusive and sometimes aggressive small people.

If eyewitnesses are to be believed, sightings of these small folk are not confined to skeletal remains. A number of people have shared experiences that suggest these beings may even endure until present day. Researchers have gathered reports of "proto-pygmies" not only from the wilds of North America, but also southern Asia, Oceania and Africa. They all seem to have some characteristics in common. They are wary and nervous, avoiding human contact. They are swift runners, nimble climbers and good swimmers. Their vocalizations suggest a primitive form of language, and they seem to live in family groups. Their diet consists of reptiles and amphibians, insects, bird eggs, small animals, fish, berries and fruit.

These descriptions have caused some researchers to identify "proto-pygmies," not with some unidentified branch of human evolution, but actually with *Australopithecus*, an extinct genus of hominids. From archaeological evidence, we know that *Australopithecus* evolved in eastern Africa around four million years ago and then spread out before becoming extinct two million years later. They were diminutive and agile, standing around 1.25 metres tall, and were fully covered with hair, like chimpanzees.

Although there is no evidence that dwarfed relatives of *Homo erectus*, like *Homo floresiensis*, or *Australopithecus* ever reached the Americas, one cannot completely discount the possibility and that these people formed the basis of First Nation tales of dwarves. After all, behind every legend there is generally a fragment of truth. Cryptozoologists will point out that 13,000 years (the date when *Homo floresiensis* supposedly went extinct) is merely a blink of an eye in geological terms, so it's possible that a North American version of Flores Man existed in small pockets into relative recent history. It is possible that they died out hundreds instead of thousands of years ago?

Speculation into these matters may seem like utter fantasy. But maybe we should keep a sliver of an open mind. Reflect back on the tiny Flores Man for a second, and consider how that discovery rattled the foundations of science. A race of dwarves had actually existed, and more than that, seemingly thrived in isolation. Suddenly, ancient legends of "little people" and "wee folk" don't seem so outlandish anymore. Fantasy emerged as fact.

Maybe one day we'll learn that diminutive people did indeed share North America with First Nations Peoples at one point. Maybe they still do.

# Chapter 18

# Adlet

~

The Inuit men struggled through a blistering world of bone white. Howling winds hurled a million specks of crystalline ice at the three desperate men, peppering their bodies with the force of a −50°C windchill. The sky could not be distinguished from the ground in the dizzying vortex of white. Fighting the gusts, the men pushed on in desperation.

Unseen, hidden by the driving snow, something stalked them.

Fear drove the men onwards even though the frigid wind and blowing snow stung their faces. Through the blasting swirls of white, they caught a brief glimpse of a dark object ahead. Moments later, the screaming started. A fearsome howl heralded the sudden attack. Slashing claws and ripping teeth spilled crimson blood against the snow. In mere seconds, the carnage was over. The Inuit hadn't even had the opportunity to raise their spears in defence.

The Inuit had good reason to fear the night. For thousands of years, from the depths of the Arctic winter's eternal night, Adlets have stalked humanity from the darkness.

In ancient times Adlets were mostly confined to the Arctic realm because of its remoteness. The area was slow to be explored by Europeans, so we have only occasional written accounts of Adlets from this region. But there is reason to believe these predators may have extended their range southward starting in the 17th century.

These canine humanoids are said to stealthily prowl through the wilderness of northern Québec and Labrador, across Canada's Arctic and up into Greenland. They are most populous around Hudson Bay, where they are also known as Erqigdlit. Adlets tower over humans, standing more than 2 metres in height and weighing 200 to 300 pounds of pure muscle. They have wolf-like heads complete with erect ears, yellow eyes, a canine snout and sharp fangs filling a wide mouth. Long arms end in sharp claws used for disembowelling prey. Adlets are covered in fur ranging from red to grey to black and have bushy wolf-like tails.

Like the wolves they resemble, Adlets are instinctively social beings that form packs. They are relentless predators that hunt as a unit, coordinating their attacks with great efficiency. While they will kill any game, including caribou and moose, they love nothing more than fresh, hot human blood and sucking marrow out of the bones of their human prey. Their howls can be heard echoing across the tundra, causing man and beast alike to shiver in fear. As night deepens, even the bravest man huddles closer to the fire.

A version of the origins of the terrifying Adlet appeared in *The Journal of American Folklore* in 1889, courtesy of Franz Boas, an ethnologist who recorded many Inuit stories and heard this particular tale in Baffin Land. This tale, often referred to as "The Girl and the Dogs," is also told by the Inuit of Greenland.

A young woman, Niviarsiang, lived with her father, Savirqong, who lamented the fact that she would not take a husband. Many young suitors attempted to woo her, but all were found wanting by the particular Niviarsiang, which earned her the name Uinigumissuitung ("she who wouldn't take a husband"). After years of rejecting all suitors, Niviarsiang further horrified her long-suffering father when she at long last married, choosing a dog, Ijirqang, for her mate. The unusual couple had ten children, five of which were purebred dogs and five that were an amalgam of man and canine, the first Adlet.

Ijirqang was a lazy cur; however, and refused to hunt to feed his large family. It fell to Savirqong, the grandfather of the yapping brood, to provide for them. Eventually Savirqong became fed up with the situation. He put the pups, dog and Adlet alike, into a boat and carried them off to a small island, and then told Ijirqang that if he and Niviarsiang wanted to eat, he would have to go to the island to get his meat daily. Too lazy to hunt, Ijirqang was forced comply. Every day, Ijirqang would hang a pair of boots around his neck, and he would swim to the island, where Savirqong would put two portions of meat, one for each of them, into the boots. One day, instead of meat, Savirqong put stones in the boots, and Ijirqang drowned under the weight.

After watching her mate sink beneath the waves and listening to his terrified final yelps, Niviarsiang became convinced that her father would next kill her children. The Adlet she sent far into the interior, to a wild, distant land beyond her father's reach. From these five Adlet an entire race sprang. As for the young dogs, Niviarsiang put them in a boat and sent them across the ocean on a journey of many, many days to a land far beyond the farthest point of land any Inuit had ever seen. These pups became the ancestors of Europeans.

Another Adlet origin myth suggests this vile race came about when a dog raped an Inuit woman. Months later, she gave birth to ten offspring, again five dogs and five Adlet. Though initially horrified at the sight of the children she had brought into the world, the woman and her husband decided to raise the babies as best they could. The Adlets matured quickly; however, and as they grew, a thirst for blood emerged. Their parents tried to restrain them, but there was no denying the Adlets' base animal instincts. One day, the Adlets savagely attacked their mother and would have killed her had her husband not fought them off and driven them far, far away into the wilderness of the interior of the country. To safeguard the five dog offspring, the mother put them onto a log and cast it out into the ocean, where it eventually reached distant shores. The dog offspring gave rise to the people of Europe.

Interestingly, similar stories about a woman who marries a dog and sires canine-human hybrid offspring are told across much of the northern reaches of North America. In Alaska, Indigenous Peoples tell of a dog named Aselu who was tied to a stick outside its owner's residence. One night, he set himself free by biting through the stick then went inside and mated with a woman. She consequently gave birth to a litter consisting of dogs and dog-like humans. You can even find eerily similar tales to that of the Adlet on the Siberian side of the Bering Strait, among the Chukchi people.

Regardless of where the tale is told, the Adlet—or whatever name these monsters are called in the local dialect—are bloodthirsty, cannibalistic warriors who attack Inuit whenever their paths cross. Adlets are inevitably victorious in these encounters, thanks to their strength and savagery and because, like werewolves, they can only be harmed by silver weapons and fire. Any attempt to flee from the Adlet is in vain as their long legs and loping gaits ensure they are faster than any human. They also have far greater endurance, enabling them to relentlessly pursue their prey for hours or even days on end. After their victims have fallen, they set upon their still warm bodies in a frenzy of claws and teeth, flaying open skin and ripping flesh from bone. When at last the Adlets' hunger is sated, little of their victims remain.

Some ethnologists believe the Adlet was nothing more than a reference to inland First Nations, with whom the Inuit occasionally warred. This is based upon interpretations of the word *adlet* hailing from root words meaning "others" or perhaps "striped ones," a possible reflection of many First Nations' penchant for facial decoration. Perhaps this is merely wishful thinking; however, a thought meant to allow us to sleep cozily in our warm beds at night. Inuit from Greenland and Baffin Land, where the Adlet was as feared as anywhere, had no First Nations neighbours. They knew something horrible and vile lurked in the darkness, something that could descend upon them at a moment's notice and slay them with barely an effort. They knew the Adlet existed and was a horrifying amalgam of man and wolf.

It's interesting that the Adlet hail from regions—Siberia, Alaska, Canada's remote north and Greenland—where strong shamanic tradition rooted in the Neolithic times survives.

Some fringe researchers postulated that perhaps rather than an actual race of man-wolves, the Adlet were shamanic enemies of the Inuit using sorcerous means to shapeshift and assume a hybrid "wolf-man" form. Or maybe the Adlet were an Arctic subtype of Sasquatch that had vaguely wolf-like features. What if, these researchers ask, these monsters were actually tribes of native lycanthropes? It's an interesting theory.

Either the existence of the Adlet is a myth, or they have blessedly retreated even farther from civilization over the last few centuries and have somehow gone unreported. When I'm tucked into bed at my cottage at night and the forest outside comes alive with unidentifiable sounds, I sleep better thinking that the former possibility is the case.

# Chapter 19

# Ogopogo

~

For more than a century and a half, since British Columbia newspapers first began committing ink to it, the notion of a lake monster—a living dinosaur, no less—hiding in the depths of Lake Okanagan has fascinated scientists, journalists, explorers, tourists and cryptozoologists alike. Even today, in the 21st century when reason rules, many serious-minded researchers continue to seek evidence that the deep, cold waters of this western lake hide a real, surviving relic of the Jurassic era.

So what's the appeal? Why are we so obsessed with the lake monster affectionately known as Ogopogo? It's a story that has many surprising twists and turns, fitting for one of the world's most astounding and perplexing phenomena.

We can't know for certain how far back into history the creature has inhabited the depths of Okanagan Lake, sating itself on fish and other aquatic prey, and the occasional unwary victim dragged screaming from the surface. But we can say for sure that the Indigenous Peoples who lived in the area have long told tales of a fell creature with a mouth of flesh-ripping teeth rising from the depths. That much is evident by the name they gave to the beast: N'ha-a-ailk, or Naitaka, meaning "lake demon."

According to First Nations lore, the creature's origins were soaked in blood and despair. In the distant past, a village wise man was murdered by a stranger said to be possessed by a devil spirit. The old man's tribe was devastated by the loss. In their grief and mourning, they called upon the gods to avenge the death of their Elder. The gods heard their prayers. Divine magic transformed the murderer into a serpent and imprisoned him in Lake Okanagan.

Naitaka didn't rest peacefully in its aquatic prison, however. From the watery depths in which it lurked, the serpent terrorized the people that resided along the lakeshore. Victims were plucked from the shore or had their canoes overturned, throwing them into the water where they were helpless. An angry creature, Naitaka churned the waters into such a fury when it travelled that waves grew high, and the winds roared. Sightings of Naitaka often heralded powerful storms and dangerous flooding, and it was believed the beast summoned these storms to blow or wash victims into its watery domain. Locals knew better than to venture onto the waters of the lake without first giving a peace offering for safe travel.

When European settlers arrived, they too developed a healthy fear of Naitaka. And why wouldn't they? According to most eyewitnesses, the creature is large—anywhere from 5 to 8 metres—and serpentine in appearance, with a frightening head that rises to a height of about 2 metres above the lake's surface. Hard-won experience taught them to be fearful of this creature born of chaos. One day, settler John McDougall headed out across the lake to help a neighbour with his haying. He climbed into his canoe and pushed off from shore with a pair of horses swimming behind. McDougall made the cardinal sin of not making any offerings to Naitaka before venturing out onto the water. He was halfway across the lake when the horses screamed in terror and suddenly disappeared, flailing and thrashing as they were dragged down by something unseen below. After that incident, armed settlers began patrolling the lakeshore to protect their families and livestock.

In 1900, 10-year-old Ruth Richardson of Okanagan Landing had an experience that haunted her into old age. She was playing on the beach in front of her house when, as she later related, "all of a sudden I heard a swish of water and it drew my attention, so I looked out on the water and here was this Ogopogo up there as big as life." She recalled its appearance vividly, even when she had greyed with age and many memories began to blur. It was dark green in colour, serpentine and had a horse-like head that it held one metre above the water. Ruth was not initially alarmed; instead, she stood rooted to the spot, too amazed by what she was seeing to move. "It was quite a way out but still and looking at me as though I was as big a curiosity to him as he was to me," she said. Moments later, while Ruth's young mind was still trying to process the experience, the serpent sank back beneath the water and disappeared. Suddenly, there came another sound of splashing water, marking the creature's return. This time, the monster was much closer and somehow more menacing. Ruth, terrified, ran to her house.

Only a year later, a Mr. Lysons was fishing near Squally Point on Lake Okanagan when something took hold of his hook and dragged both him and his boat through the water. Whatever it was, the creature was large and incredibly powerful. Lysons had fished the lake for many years and had never encountered a fish with that much strength. Thankfully, before the boat was swamped, the line snapped.

It was in the 1920s, however, that the monster of Lake Okanagan really entered the spotlight and became an international sensation. The process began in 1924 when the original name, Naitaka, was replaced by the more whimsical Ogopogo, a name coined by local journalist Ronald Kenvyn and inspired by a popular music hall tune of the era ("The Ogo-Pogo, the Funny Fox-Trot," which tells of a banjo-playing monster from Hindustan). Two years later, there was a mass sighting that captured newspaper headlines across North America. On September 16, 1926, dozens of people—in no fewer than 30 vehicles—saw an immense, unidentifiable serpent-like animal near Okanagan Mission Beach.

Newspaper accounts of this sighting captured the popular imagination. In America, it caused sportsmen in Washington, Oregon and California to organize hunting parties that resolved to hunt and kill Ogopogo. This was the biggest, most exotic game of all, and they meant to mount its head on a wall. British Columbians were incensed by these plans and saw to it that the Americans knew they were unwelcome. Thankfully, nothing came of these bloodthirsty ambitions, but locals remained concerned that, in the future, others would attempt to hunt and kill a creature they had become fiercely territorial over. To ward off potential hunters, locals began circulating positive stories about Ogopogo that were picked up by wire services and published by newspapers all over the continent. The plan seemed to work, as the terrifying Naitaka evolved almost overnight into the friendly, if enigmatic, Ogopogo.

A new threat against Ogopogo emerged a few decades later, however. On July 18, 1950, three men were working in an apple orchard at Carris Landing when Ogopogo surfaced just offshore. Though the creature showed no sign of aggression, the men grabbed rifles and began firing at it. Several rounds struck home and the panicked creature dove to escape. An hour later, Ogopogo was seen heading north "and churning up the water as if in distress." This was too much for the people of British Columbia. Concerned citizens put pressure on the government to protect the lake serpent, and their voices were heard. Under the Fisheries Act, it became illegal to kill Ogopogo.

Ogopogo was becoming a tourist attraction. In 1951, Gilbert Seabrook, the manager of a radio station in Vernon, BC, copyrighted the name Ogopogo and two years later transferred the copyright to the citizens of that community.

So what exactly is Ogopogo? This vivid description comes from a Mr. Kray, who sighted the beast on July 2, 1947. According to his account, Ogopogo has "a long sinuous body, 30 feet [10 metres] in length, consisting of about five undulations, apparently separated from each other by about a two-foot [60-centimetre] space, in which that part of the undulations would have been underwater." Kray went on to add that, "there appeared to be a forked tail, of which only one-half came above the water. From time to time the whole thing submerged and came up again."

Let's also consider the testimony of Mrs. B. Clark. Hers is of particular relevance because there has never been a sighting closer. She was swimming one morning in mid-July in 1974 when something large and heavy bumped up against her legs. Quite naturally, she was startled and looked about to see what it could have been. Clark was stunned to see a 2-metre-long coil or hump, more than one metre above the water, travelling away from her at a leisurely pace. As the water was very clear, she could make out a dark grey body just below the surface. This creature's body was smooth and hairless with stripes running down the back and a forked, horizontal tail resembling that of a whale. As the hump descended, the tail rose, until its flukes rose above the surface—again, like a whale. She estimated the creature to be 8 to 10 metres long, but only 1.2 metres across. "It acted more like a whale than a fish, but I have never seen a whale that skinny and snaky-looking before," Clark said. "It was definitely not reptilian, and I'm sure it wasn't a fish."

Most descriptions of Ogopogo over the years are consistent with those left by Kray and Clark. Generally, Ogopogo is reported as having an elongated, snake-like body with dark green, black or brown skin, flippers, a split tail and a horse-like head that rises out of the water to a height of 1.8 to 2 metres on a long neck. Some people have described serrations on its back and/or a mane on its head. Ogopogo is a large creature, measuring anywhere from 5 to 8 metres long, and displaying undulating humps.

Skeptics will posit that people aren't actually seeing a monster at all, but rather something mundane, such as a large fish, perhaps a catfish or muskie or even ducks swimming in a row. This seems remarkably unlikely, and no known animal satisfactorily explains away the countless accounts that have emerged over the years. Most believers are of the mind that Ogopogo is a plesiosaur, an enormous aquatic reptile said to have been extinct for 65 million years.

Some others hold to the theory put forward by cryptozoologist Gary Mangiacopra and University of Chicago biologist Roy Mackel that Ogopogo is a zeuglodon, a primitive form of whale that supposedly went extinct. Certainly the description corresponds closely with the zeuglodon, as does the method of locomotion; whereas snakes and eels undulate horizontally, zeuglodons like other aquatic mammals, would have undulated vertically, just as the many eyewitnesses claim Ogopogo swims through the water.

The zeuglodon is the same prehistoric predator that many have linked to Caddy, the sea monster of the British Columbia coast (for more details on this creature, see Chapter Five). Zoologist Ed Bousfield agrees that these two monsters, Caddy and Ogopogo, belong to the same species. He puts forward the idea that both animals may have eaten salmon, and that Ogopogo may have routinely followed salmon up the Columbia River into Lake Okanagan. He postulates that several individuals became trapped in the lake when dams were built that have blocked direct access to the ocean.

Biologists agree that at 13 kilometres long, and just over 400 kilometres deep, Lake Okanagan is indeed large enough to allow a colony of predominantly underwater-based creatures to survive and thrive within it.

Skeptics want proof, not theories and possibilities. Some intriguing evidence has in fact surfaced over the years to go along with eyewitness accounts, which run into the hundreds. In 1968, a man named Art Folden filmed what he believed was

Ogopogo swimming across Lake Okanagan. Though the film is grainy and taken at considerable distance thanks to the limitations of home movie cameras of the day, many experts who have studied it believe it is both authentic and captures something unusual. Indeed, the film garnered enough interest that it spawned a number of expensive expeditions using a variety of hi-tech equipment to scour the lake for an anomalous creature lurking within it. Thus far these searches have come up empty. Then, in July 1989, Ogopogo was captured on film a second time. This film was sent to the National Geographic Society in Washington, DC, for analysis. The results were inconclusive but labeled "interesting" by the experts that studied it.

Lack of solid evidence hasn't deterred thousands of tourists from descending on Lake Okanagan each year in hopes of sighting this elusive Ogopogo. The monster of the past, at one time feared and hunted, has been transformed into a whimsical creature that serves as a local mascot and is protected by legislation. It wouldn't be a stretch to say that Ogopogo is now beloved by locals and rivals Nessie of Scotland's Loch Ness for international acclaim.

As to what Ogopogo might be—surviving creatures from prehistory or something entirely unknown to science—the answer still eludes us.

# Chapter 20

# Manipogo and Winnipogo

~

Apprehension gripped the reporters as they shone their flashlights into the lakeside cave. The entrance was semi-flooded, but the floor rose as the cavern stretched deep back into the cliff-face. The journalists were excited and frightened at the same time; excited by the possibility that they had found the lair of the legendary lake monster, and frightened that the creature might be home and may not take kindly to being disturbed.

Cautiously, they entered the cave, their lights flashing over rough walls and a ceiling 3 metres above. As they ventured deeper, the back wall came into view with no sign of a massive reptilian monster. Hundreds of bones—of fish, small mammals and unidentifiable larger creatures—lay scattered across the sandy floor. What truly caught their attention, however, were the sweeping tracks of a heavy serpentine animal that apparently had been lying in the sand and then slipped out into the lake.

This evidence led the journalists to believe they had found the lair of Manipogo, a serpent-like monster that had ruled over Lake Manitoba for centuries...and, if modern-day cryptozoologists are to be believed, perhaps even more many millennia.

Manipogo—a name inspired by the famed Ogopogo, the monster of British Columbia's Lake Okanagan—is the moniker given to the mystery beast that allegedly lives in Lake Manitoba. The local Indigenous Peoples know all about this slithering, serpentine beast of the deep. They have legends going back centuries that tell of a gargantuan snake that slides beneath the waters of the lake, prowling for victims to temporarily sate a ravenous hunger. They know that to hunt this creature is futile. When it wishes to be seen, it rises from the water, oftentimes in a flurry of violence that leaves no eyewitnesses. When it chooses to be elusive, it simply slips beneath the waves of this deep lake.

Yet, despite the elusiveness Indigenous storytellers speak of, since the 1800s dozens, perhaps even hundreds, of people claim to have seen Manipogo. Almost always they describe a serpentine creature with a black or brown glossy hide and a number of humps that show above the water. The creature measures anywhere between 4 and 17 metres long, though most observers report something in the 10-metre range. It has a small, flat head, sometimes likened to that of a sheep, from which sprouts its most distinctive feature: a single horn said to resemble that of a rhinoceros.

The earliest recorded sighting was by a Hudson's Bay Company fur trader back in 1909. Three decades later, in 1935, a timber inspector named C. F. Ross came forward and claimed to have seen a creature that, until then, was generally considered to be nothing more than an Indigenous legend, if it was known at all. Ross said it resembled a dinosaur, even though he must have realized how ridiculous that sounded.

Then followed a flurry of sightings from the late 1940s through to the 1960s, beginning in 1948 with C.P. Alric who, like Ross, said the creature resembled a dinosaur. He said the monster's head rose 2 metres out of the water atop a long, thin neck, then opened a mouth lined with sharp teeth and gave a "prehistoric type of dinosaur cry." There was some hysteria in 1957 after two fishermen saw a giant serpent-like monster. When local newspapers picked up the story, they dubbed the monster Manipogo—a name that has since stuck. There was such interest at the time that a group of journalists organized an expedition of sorts to get to the bottom of the stories and perhaps even find Manipogo. Although the lake monster was never seen, the expedition did find the cave they believed might have been its lair.

James McLeod, Chairman of the Department of Zoology at the University of Manitoba, launched another expedition in 1960. His interest was spurred by the reports of almost two dozen people who were picnicking along the shores of Lake Manitoba on July 24 of that year. All saw the same massive serpentine creature, with humps that broke the lake's glass-like surface, swimming leisurely past. McLeod's expedition was as fruitless as its predecessor three years earlier, but McLeod remained convinced something lurked within the lake and continued his research for years afterward.

In 1962 came the first photo of Manipogo. One of a very few to have ever been taken of the cryptid, it does indeed appear to show a mysterious and unidentifiable creature. Many experts who have studied the picture are intrigued by it, and thus far no one has been able to prove it's a hoax. If it's a fake, it's a clever one.

Manipogo may have become shy with all the attention because it seemed to lie low for a few decades. Some began to wonder if the creature had gone or died...if it had ever existed at all. And then, towards the end of the century, Manipogo suddenly returned. In 1989, Minneapolis native Sean Smith and his family were visiting Lake Manitoba on a camping trip. While encamped at Shallow Point, the entire clan saw something break the surface of the lake about 25 metres offshore. They watched as "many humps" slid noiselessly through the water for several long minutes before finally disappearing below the surface. A decade later, in 1997, Manipogo caused a panicked evacuation of the water at Lundar Beach Campground when a large reptile head suddenly surfaced near swimmers. The head quickly disappeared, and officials dismissed it as a floating log, but no log could be found afterwards.

While many of the eyewitnesses over the years might conceivably mistake a floating log for a aquatic monster, Keith Haden is not one of them. A commercial fisherman originally from Newfoundland who began plying his trade on Lake Manitoba, he's spent a lifetime on the waters and is intimately familiar with marine life, both freshwater and saltwater. As a result, the events he claims took place in 2004 should carry considerable weight. Haden had cast his fishing nets earlier on the day in question and was returning to retrieve them, anticipating a good haul for his efforts. He was stunned and angry when the nets were finally pulled into the boat; they had been torn up in a manner similar to what a shark might do. Worse, the fish trapped in the nets were torn in half by what seemed like huge bites. All that remained were heads with bulging eyes stuck in the netting.

Other reliable eyewitnesses surfaced in 2011 when on several occasions security officers patrolling flooded residential areas and cottages saw several humps surfacing offshore of Laurentia Beach, Marshy Point and Scotch Bay. The humps seemed to belong to something extremely large, estimated to be as much as 13 metres long and remaining on the surface for several minutes before disappearing. Some researchers have suggested the widespread flooding that year somehow disturbed Manipogo and caused an unusual slew of sightings.

Manipogo has become such a part of local lore that St. Laurent, a village on the south shores of Lake Manitoba, holds an annual Manipogo Festival in March. But it's believed Manipogo doesn't belong just to the people residing along the shores of Lake Manitoba. Because Lake Manitoba is linked with Lake Winnipegosis, it seems likely that the lake monster said to dwell in the latter lake—named Winnipogo—belongs to the same species of Manipogo.

Winnipogo has a history just as long as its neighbouring lake monster, and just like Manipogo it has roots in Indigenous tradition. In the early decades of the 20th century, a man named Oscar Frederickson wrote an extensive report on his knowledge of the huge lake monster lurking in the cold depths of Lake Winnipegosis. He was spurred by a childhood experience that left an indelible impression on his young mind and created a fascination that endured throughout his life.

"In 1903, I lived with my parents on Red Deer Point, Lake Winnipegosis," Frederickson's writings begin. "Our house was situated about 200 metres from the shore. About a mile south of our place lived a man by the name of Ferdinand Stark. One day Stark was down by the lakeshore when he saw

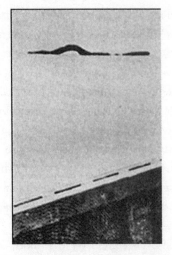

what he thought was a huge creature in the lake. It was moving northward along the shore, a short distance out."

Stark wanted someone else to see the creature, so he ran to the Frederickson homestead. He arrived "very much excited and breathing heavily," but by then the creature had disappeared. Instead, he related the experience. "All I could see of the creature was its big head sticking out of the water, and it was very dark or black in color. A number of gulls followed it and kept flying down to it as if they were picking at it."

Another man, Valentine McKay, later related his own experience with the monster of Lake Winnipegosis. In September 1909, he was standing on shore making a campfire when he heard a "rumbling sound like distant thunder." He looked out onto the glassy lake and saw "a huge creature propelling itself on the surface of the water about 400 metres out from shore. A large part must have been submerged, judging by the great disturbance of the water around it. The creature's dark skin glistened in the autumn sun, and I estimated it was moving at the rate of two or three miles [3 or 5 kilometres] an hour. As I watched it, a member of the body shot up about four feet [1.2 metres], vertically, out of the water. This portion seemed to have something to do with the creature's method of locomotion."

McKay watched as it disappeared behind Sugar Island with a number of gulls hovering above, following it as it swam out of sight.

McKay apparently described the creature to a geologist, and the geologist said that, in his opinion, it might have been a "remaining specimen of a prehistoric animal that was once plentiful." Presumably, the geologist had some knowledge of fossils in order to make such a statement.

Frederickson was convinced that both men genuinely believed they had seen something truly unusual and that neither was exaggerating their claims. He notes: "A great many people will think these two men just made up a story about seeing some strange animal or creature in Lake Winnipegosis. But, it is hardly probable that both men would think up a yarn about the gulls. Stark and McKay never met, as far as I could find out."

In 1934, Captain Sandy Vance, a lifetime tugboat captain on Lake Winnipegosis and Lake Winnipeg, saw a "huge creature a short distance off shore." It was the biggest living creature he had ever seen in water, keeping in mind he had seen a great many moose and bear swimming in the lakes.

Dr. James McLeod of the University of Manitoba took an interest in Winnipogo as part of his study of Manipogo. He was excited to learn that a huge spinal vertebra of an unknown creature was supposedly found on the shores of the lake in the 1930s. The bone was lost in a fire, but a wooden model had been made beforehand and was presented to McLeod.

In Mcleod's judgment, the bone resembled that of the prehistoric, whale-like zeuglodon. Sadly, he was forced to admit that without the original as proof, the model was little more than an enticing curiosity.

In the years since Frederickson wrote his report, sightings of Winnipogo have become rarer. All who do see it say the same thing: The creature, like Manipogo, is well over 7 metres long and is serpentine in shape, and it swims with humps undulating in the water.

Real or imagined, fact or fiction, Manipogo and Winnipogo remain a part of local lore. These serpent-like beasts hunt the deeps and shores with sharp teeth swimming into our imagination.

# Chapter 21

# Nuk-luk

~

Canada's North is an unforgiving place, a bitter landscape where inhabitants—human and animal alike—eke out an equally difficult existence. Yet this cold and harsh region may be the last refuge of an ancient species, the mysterious and widely feared Nuk-luk, or "man of the bush."

Also known as Nakani ("bad Indian") or Bushmen, Nuk-luk are hairy and powerful wild men that inhabit the deep woods, blustery wind-carved badlands and rugged highlands of the Northwest Territories, Yukon and Alaska. Standing about 2 metres tall, they are covered in short, dark hair, with red or yellow eyes below heavy brows and above a wide nose. They have long, thickly muscled arms that end in clawed nails on well-weathered hands.

Indigenous lore paints a vivid picture of these bestial men. Generally nocturnal, they follow a yearly cycle similar to that of bears—active throughout the spring and summer, then ravenously feasting in autumn to build up fat stores before spending much of the harsh winter in a cave or an underground den. Nuk-luk are swift runners, which comes in handy when escaping with dried salmon stolen from the smokehouses of the First Nations communities.

Though generally elusive and shy, Nuk-luk will either flee or throw rocks and sticks when threatened. Some stories tell of Nuk-luk kidnapping women and children or assaulting hunters who trespass on their territory. And then there are worse stories, the ones that make the Nuk-luk so widely feared. While most Bushmen gather and hunt to sustain themselves, a few choose another source of sustenance: humans. Perhaps they do so after suffering such desperate privations that they have no other choice but to emerge from their backwoods domain to hunt people. But Indigenous lore says some turn to eating humans for pleasure, the thrill of the hunt made all the more exhilarating for seeing terror in the eyes of their victims. There are even stories of Nuk-luk having hypnotic powers, which they use to draw in victims or, more benevolently, to erase the memory of anyone they encounter.

While Nuk-luk range stretches across two territories and one American state, one location has become synonymous with the Bushman and its worst, most violent tendencies. That region is the Northwest Territory's Nahanni Valley, ominously nicknamed The Headless Valley or Deadman Valley. For more than two hundred years, this rugged river valley has been the site of numerous strange human disappearances, with dozens of documented vanishings recorded since 1904. The bodies of at least four of the missing people have later turned up without their heads. The folklore of Indigenous Peoples has the Nahanni Valley as the fiercely guarded domain of Nuk-luk, leading many to surmise the disappearances were at the hands of these ill-tempered wild men. The mystery has never been solved.

One mystery that has been solved, at least according to some cryptozoologists, is the identity of the Nuk-luk. These researchers believe the Nuk-luk represent a relic population of Neandertals that still roam parts of the world, leaving tracks and legends of degenerate, primitive "bushmen." *Homo neaderthalensis* was closely related to modern humans. They shared 99.7 percent of our DNA, making modern humans more closely related to "cavemen" than to their closest non-human relative, the chimpanzee, which shares 98.8 percent of its DNA with us.

Nevertheless, despite genetic intimacy, there are many notable differences between Neandertals and modern humans. Neandertals were stockier and much stronger, with wide chests and powerful arms and hands. They had larger, broader noses, reduced chins, heavy brow ridges and bigger eyes that, combined with evidence in the cranial cavity, suggests their vision was superior to ours. Males averaged 2 metres tall with shorter legs and bigger bodies designed to preserve heat in the cold climates they inhabited. As part of their adaptation to the cold, it also seems probable that Neandertals were furred. In their book *The 10,000 Year Explosion*, authors Gregory Cochran and Henry Harpending explain, "Chimpanzees have ridges on their finger bones that stem from the way that they clutch their mothers' fur as infants. Modern humans don't have these ridges, but Neandertal do." In addition, Cochran and Harpending point out that while Neandertals undoubtedly made and used tools, thus far there has been no evidence of clothes-making tools—strongly suggesting that the species had to be furred to survive in their environment.

Anthropologists tell us that Neandertals were a very successful, adaptive species. They seemed to have appeared first in Europe (where their fossils were first discovered in Germany about 150 years ago) and later expanded into southwest, central and northern Asia. Neandertals were contemporaries of modern humans and shared Europe with them for several thousand years until the Neandertals died out around 30,000 years ago.

The question is, just how adaptive were they? Could some Neandertals have avoided extinction and survived thousands of years in isolated pockets in remote areas around the globe? Cryptozoologists point to "The Epic of Gilgamesh," the ancient Babylonian story as "proof" that Neandertals survived into relatively recent times. This story, written 4000 years ago, focuses on the hero Gilgamesh and his friend Enkidu— a hairy and powerful wild man who was "trained" (i.e. civilized) and served as King Gilgamesh's champion in battle. Some believe Enkidu was, in fact, a Neandertal.

Furthermore, folklore from cultures the world over speaks of beings remarkably similar in appearance to Neandertals, most notably the Almasty of the Caucasus region of southern Russia. Modern sightings suggest some of these beings might have endured into recent times, and perhaps still exist in places such as Canada's north. Researchers suggest that Neandertals may have crossed the land bridge from the Eurasia landmass thousands of years in the past and established themselves in wilderness areas where they cling to existence today.

One piece of evidence they point to in order to link the Nuk-luk with Neandertals is the similarity in the footprints left behind after Bushman encounters with those found in the floors of prehistoric Neandertal-inhabited caves in Europe.

The two are identical. More evidence can be found in the physical descriptions left by eyewitnesses over the years.

The Nuk-luk made a series of appearances in the spring and early summer of 1964. One day in April, John Baptiste, along with several other Indigenous men from Fort Laird in the Yukon, was trapping in the wilderness highlands near the junction of the frigid Laird and South Nahanni Rivers when the group spotted a hairy figure in the trees. The figure was powerfully built, with long, stringy hair that flowed past its muscled shoulders and a long, dark beard. Despite the chilly spring weather, the man wore not a stitch of clothing. The trappers, knowing well the legend of the Nuk-luk, felt fear welling up within them and reflexively gripped their rifles tighter. The hairy man, seemingly sensing their presence for the first time, uttered a low guttural growl and then fled deeper back into the protective folds of the forest.

Two months later there was a report of a similar creature near Fort Simpson in the Northwest Territories. One evening, at about 9:00 PM, a dog belonging to 14-year-old Jerry began barking. The dog was clearly agitated by something; its bark was incessant and higher-pitched than normal. When the boy and his father went out with a flashlight to find out what was wrong, they were surprised to see a hominid creature covered with coarse black hair on its head, chest, arms and legs. A scraggly brown beard reached all the way down to its broad waist. Unlike the bushman seen in April, this one wore clothing in the form of a piece of moose skin wrapped around its waist. Clenched in a large, dark hand was a menacing stone club.

The Nuk-luk was startled by the sudden appearance of Jerry and his father. It stood frozen in the glare of the flashlights for a moment and then bolted in panic, racing across the property on muscled legs and bolting across the road in front of the house where several bystanders also spotted it. A number of men gave chase, but the Nuk-luk dashed into the bush and disappeared amidst the trees and bushes in an almost preternatural way, easily losing its pursuers.

There was also a flurry of Nuk-luk sightings across the border in Alaska during the 1960s. One October day in 1960, Paul Peters was walking his dogs along the banks of the Yukon River near Ruby, Alaska. All was well at first, but then Peters' dogs began whining and acting strangely. The hair on their shoulders stood on end, their tails tucked between their legs, and they uncharacteristically clung to their owner's side. Peters crinkled his nose as a musky odor assailed his nostrils. Then he saw the cause of the smell and his dogs' discomfort: Walking along a rocky beach towards him was a Nuk-luk, all muscles, black hair and glowering eyes. The bushman towered over Peters; he estimated it stood well over 2 metres tall. Now as uneasy as his dogs, Peters gathered them up and beat a hasty retreat. A couple of years later, an Alaskan First Nations woman saw a Nuk-luk hovering in the wood-line near her home, silently watching her with dark eyes clouded by a heavy brow and a mane of wild hair. Then, in 1970, seven residents of the village of Nulato were attacked by a Nuk-luk while on a hunting expedition. They were camped along the banks of the Koyukuk River about 20 miles north of its confluence with the Yukon, when a hail of rocks and tree limbs rained down on them from the woods. Strange grunting and barks accompanied the assault. Because they were far from civilization, the hunters were convinced the attacker was a Bushman.

John Bernard Bourne wrote a fascinating article, "Glimpsing the Bushman," for the March 3, 2003 edition of *Maclean's* magazine wherein he detailed an improbable modern-day encounter with a Nuk-Luk.

Bourne had moved with his wife and young daughter to Rae Lake, a small isolated community in the Northwest Territories where he lived among the Dogrib people and immersed himself in their culture. Bourne was entranced with their way of life and, despite being a Caucasian, was welcomed by the tribe. He went on caribou hunts, attended community feasts and participated in their ceremonial singing and dancing. It was while listening to folktales that he first learned of the Nuk-luk, a fearsome entity the Dogrib referred to as the Bushman.

"According to the Dogrib people there exists a creature known as the Bushman. It is tall and hairy and lurks in the bush ready to abduct anyone travelling alone. Those who have been taken by the Bushman are usually never seen again, and if they are, they are found mute and mentally deranged," Bourne writes. "As an outsider, this story sounded a lot like a cross between BC's Sasquatch and eastern Canada's Windigo; but for the Dogribs it is something to be taken very seriously."

Bourne found the perpetual darkness of the northern winter, which lasts from the end of October to March, hard to grow accustomed to. He could easily see how a mystery creature could remain hidden in the northern wilderness, with its six months of endless night, sparse population and vast expanses of trackless taiga and tundra, but he never expected to see one. As much as Bourne was a part of the tribe, he still believed most of their tales were just that—tales. That notion ended suddenly one winter day. Bourne writes:

> It was when the daylight was beginning to reappear that I saw the Bushman. It was the middle of March and I was driving with my wife and a friend on the winter road (the ice road that is open about six weeks every year to bring in food and supplies). We were

*caught in a blizzard and our visibility had deterio-
rated to nothing. We were stuck on the frozen, endless
white of Faber Lake, halfway between Gameti and
Rae-Edzo (which means "in the middle of nowhere").
It was just a flash. In fact, I would have thought it
was an illusion brought on by the snow, but the other
two people with me saw it as well."*

*It was tall and hairy, running on its hind legs. The
hair was long and hung from its body in an unkempt
and wild manner. It was gone before we could say
anything. My friend, who was driving shouted,
"What was that?" But we all knew. We tried to push
our original instinct away and rationalize it as something else. But we couldn't.*

On several occasions, Bourne later shared the experience
with friends and family back in his native Ontario. No one
believed him. Some thought he was fabricating a tall tale.
Others tried to rationalize it as a bear. It was only the Dogrib
people who accepted the story at face value. Whenever he
shared the experience among his northern neighbors, they
would simply nod solemnly. The Nuk-luk, to them, was a real
as the squirrel in the tree in your yard or the birds eating at
the feeder outside your window. Bourne continued:

*This past fall, a story began circulating around our
village. The wise ones were giving everybody fair
warnings—they had a premonition that the Bushman
would be abducting somebody this year. We were
warned to be careful and not go walking by ourselves
into the bush. I was surprised by how I reacted. Three
years ago I would have laughed and made fun of it.
Now, I just accepted the warning and kept it at the
back of my mind....Logically, I know there is no*

> *Bushman. It makes no sense and defies any type of scientific evidence…but I did see something on that winter road.*

The sighting had a profound impact on Bourne. As much as he knew the Nuk-luk shouldn't exist. He also knows—as fantastic as it sounds—that it does. He concludes:

> *Winter is here again, and the long darkness gives you time to think. Tales of the Bushman do not really pervade your thoughts during the times of daylight. But now, it almost seems plausible. Every night, when I put my baby daughter to bed, I lie beside her, singing songs and telling stories. When she falls asleep I used to creep out quietly and sit with my wife in the other room. Lately, however, I find myself staying longer, well after she has fallen into a deep slumber. I feel this subconscious urge to guard and watch over her, and protect her from the bushman. Just in case.*

That's the thing about the Nuk-luk. You instinctively believe it can't exist, shouldn't exist. We're raised by science to believe it's impossible for a Neanderthaloid wildman to prowl the wilds of northern Canadian. Yet there's always the nagging doubt that there might just be something out there, just beyond the edge of the campfire's light. And then when you see one—when the moon emerges from behind a grey cloud to illuminate the hairy torso, muscled limbs and prehistoric face in stark clarity—you're left with the uncomfortable realization that all you've known and believed for your entire life may be horribly wrong.

Does the Nuk-luk haunt Canada's northern wilderness, or does it just haunt our nightmares?

# Chapter 22

# Wendigo

~

The Coppermine Expedition of 1819–22 was seemingly cursed from the very beginning. The overland British expedition was organized by the Royal Navy and had as its goal the exploration of Canada's northern coast in an attempt discover and map the Northwest Passage. Led by Sir John Franklin, it was plagued by poor planning and inclement weather that saw the men endure horrific privations. They reached the Arctic coast, but by then food supplies had been exhausted and the expedition made a desperate retreat across uncharted territory in a state of virtual starvation. The men resorted to eating lichen, boiled boot leather and the remains of wolf kills. Men began to die.

At one point three invalid men—Hood, Richardson and Hepburn—had to be left behind. The expedition continued on, but soon four more men claimed they could go no further and elected to return to the invalid camp. Only one managed to make it back to the camp, an Indigenous man named Michael Teroahaute. He brought with him fresh meat, which Teroahaute explained was from the corpse of a wolf that had been gored by a caribou. The men in camp cooked the meat and ravenously devoured it, but even in their extreme hunger they remarked on its unusual taste and consistency.

Over the next few days, the men became concerned by Teroahaute's increasingly erratic behavior. He was growing aggressive, was always heavily armed and would disappear for periods of time but always refuse to say where he went. Worse, while they were growing hungrier and weaker, Teroahaute showed few signs of diminishing health. The invalid men began to suspect Teroahaute had killed the three men who had turned back with him, and that he was disappearing from camp to feed on their corpses.

Then, one day, Hood was found shot while Richardson and Hepburn had briefly been away from camp. They now knew beyond a doubt that they were in grave danger. Teroahaute insisted that the man had shot himself, but the angle of the bullet made that extremely unlikely.

Teroahaute's companions were aware of the First Nation's belief that once a man had tasted human flesh, he developed a craving for it and could be satisfied with nothing else. He would become a Wendigo, a malevolent, cannibalistic spirit of great power and even greater hunger for human flesh. Worse still, the Wendigo could possess people, often when they were asleep, and transform them into a violent, cannibalistic monster that was a mirror of itself. Fearing for his life, Richardson shot and killed Terohaute before the transformation to man-eating monstrosity was complete.

The form Teroahaute would have taken had he completed the dire transformation is uncertain, as Wendigo vary widely in appearance. Typically, they take on the form gaunt, starved-looking giants. The emaciation belies a terrible strength, for a Wendigo can crush a skull as easily as we would a strawberry or rip limbs from a body with a casual flick of its wrist. Its head may look entirely human, save for feral-looking eyes and lips that quiver with maddening hunger, or it may resemble a wild animal—typically an elk with a gore-spattered rack of horns, but perhaps also a bear or wolf or even a hairy, bestial man. In some stories, the Wendigo is even more terrifying to behold—an emaciated body with bones that poke through sallow skin, glowing eyes, yellow fangs or broken teeth, blue tongue that flicks out from between blood-dripping lips and long legs that end in hooves or blackened, frostbitten feet.

Typically one becomes a Wendigo by being driven to cannibalism by privation or derangement, and oftentimes before succumbing, they will mutter of spirits that haunt their dreams or whisper in the wind, compelling them into the desperate act of feasting on another human being. It is said that when people start to turn Wendigo, after hours or days of increased madness, they hear the "sound of ice pressured, scraped and scrunched inside their body." An afflicted person draws one final breath and then screams as the transformation begins. After sating its hunger for human flesh, the newly risen Wendigo heads out into the wilderness in search of other individuals to possess and compel into cannibalism, thereby propagating the fell species.

Those who were suspected of being Wendigo were quickly killed. They were then decapitated and sometimes would have their legs bound or even amputated to prevent them from rising from the grave and going on rampages of mayhem and slaughter. Such killings were not confined to ancient history. As we will soon see, they continued into the 20th century with a startling number from around Kenora, Ontario.

Kenora, in the northwestern part of the province near the border with Manitoba, has the unfortunate distinction of being known as the "Wendigo Capital of the World," as a result of the numerous tales of Wendigo in this heavily forested region. Indeed, English horror writer Algernon Blackwood set his celebrated terror tale *The Wendigo* in Rat Portage (as Kenora was known prior to 1905) after being inspired—in the most gruesome of ways—during an 1898 visit.

Blackwood missed out on one of the most horrific true Wendigo stories by only a year. On November 2, 1899, the headline of the *Medicine Hat Weekly News* screamed: "Killed a Wendigo: Two Cat Lake Indians to Be Tried in Winnipeg for Murdering Their Chief." Readers anticipated a tale of tragedy, horror and gripping drama. They were not disappointed.

The tale begins with the arrest of two Indigenous men from Cat Lake in northern Ontario by North-West Mounted Police officer R.G. Chamberlain and A.B.J. Bannatyre, the Indian agent in Lac Seul. Their crime, as the headlines gave away, was the murder of their chief, Abwassakehmig.

According to the testimony of the culprits, their chief had been seduced by an evil spirit and was being transformed into a monster. Hunger became a constant sensation for the aging man, and only with the consuming of human flesh would he be free of the urges. He grew feral and was constantly raving. Everyone knew it was only a matter of time before Abwassakehmig could no longer deny the urges that were tempting him to sample the flesh of his tribesmen. In the moments before he finally lost sanity for good, the chief begged to be killed and even demonstrated where he should be shot.

"The council of the tribe was called and they discussed the matter for two days, when they arrived at the conclusion that the chief's orders would have to be obeyed," the newspaper reported. "After he was dead, wood was heaped upon his body and the fire kept going for two days, thereby, according to the belief of the Indians, thoroughly destroying the evil spirit of their chief."

The newspaper pointed out how traditionalist and superstitious the men were as a result of their isolated community, that they had never seen a train before and only one had even see a horse or cow. To such people, the Wendigo was very real, a predator in their midst that had to be killed before it could go on a bloody rampage.

The year 1906 was one year of privation for the Ojibwe of the Kenora region. Game was so scarce that people of the Sucker clan of Sandy Lake were reduced to gnawing on rawhide and eating pine cones and moss in order to stave of starvation. Soon, they were too weak to even attempt to hunt. Then, to compound the misery, the village was hit with the flu, and people began to drop.

One day, a young woman named Wahsakapeequay was struck by a lingering madness and mindlessness. She tossed and turned with terrible pangs, her spasms becoming increasingly painful. In her lucid moments,Wahsakapeequay begged her mother to end her suffering, to relieve her of the misery that could only result in death. Tribal shaman Jack Fiddler sought direction from his dreams and visions. When he came out if his dream trance, he knew what must be done. Wahsakapeequay would have to be killed before she turned Wendigo. The very whisper of Wendigo was so terrifying to the people of Sandy Lake that they didn't think twice about murdering a helpless young woman.

But Wendigo wasn't confined merely to the dark forests and dismal swamps around Kenora. Indeed, they could be found as far north as the Arctic, as far east as Québec, and west throughout Manitoba and occasionally on the Plains. The *Regina Standard* for September 20, 1899, followed the trial of two other First Nations men, named Napaysoosis and Payoo, who were accused of killing someone possessed by Wendigo. The story begins the previous winter, when the Indigenous community of 32 was living in the Bald Hills, 120 kilometres west of Lesser Slave Lake. The people were close to destitution, living in two drafty shacks and two teepees.

At the height of the winter, when nights were long and dark, game was scarce and desperation was at its height, a member of the tribe, Louison Moostoos, began to unravel. He told several members of the clan he was afraid an evil spirit was corrupting him and, as he was losing the ability to resist, he felt he was on the verge of turning *sehtiko*, or "cannibal." In the event that he did fall, Moostoos pleaded for Napaysoosis and Payoo to kill him, as he was terrified he would kill his own children.

> *During the last day and night I saw Moostoos was not looking as usual. His eyes were rolling and glittering, and he seemed afraid to look anyone in the face, and he was all the time muttering to himself. On one occasion he said: "I look upon these children as young moose, and long to eat them," explained Napaysoosis. I was absent from the shack part of the*

*day, and when I came back towards evening,
Moostoos looked wilder and more dangerous than
ever, and it was clear to all present that he was becoming a wehtiko [wendigo].*

The clan members were now gripped with fear. At any moment Moostoos might transform into a bestial man-eater and slay them all in a crimson orgy of blood and violence. They tried to use sorcery to cure the afflicted man, but without success. During the incantation, Moostoos went wild. His arms flailed about, forcing four men to pin him, and through lips flecked with spittle, he screamed, "If I get up I will kill you all tonight." At one point, he somehow managed to break free and jump to his feet, eyes blazing with madness. "Fear, intense, blind fear, took hold of us," related Napaysoosis. In desperation, four men tackled the raving man and managed to overpower him, pulling him back down to the ground. "Moostoos struggled fearfully, throwing his head about and grinding his teeth, and twice he tried to bite me, tearing my coat," Napaysoosis recalled.

Everyone now knew that Moostoos was almost gone and that the evil had almost assumed total control of his body. With his mind irrecoverably altered, it was now just a matter of time before his physical form changed as well. When that happened, they would be helpless, and all would be killed. There was now only one thing left for them to do: Kill Moostoos first. All the male members of the tribe took turns attacking the crazed man, first with an axe, striking him several times and splitting his skull, then with a knife, driving it into his belly to gut him.

Even when Moostoos no longer moved and his body had cooled to the touch, the people were still gripped with fear. They expected the Wendigo to reanimate the corpse and cause it to rise up again. To forestall that, Moostoos' legs were chained to two pickets driven into the ground so that the body could not get up and chase after them, and finally, they cut off his head with an axe so that if he got up, he could not eat them. It was only after the sun had risen and Moostoos still lay cold and motionless that the community finally felt relief.

Incredibly, despite admitting to the slaying, Napaysoosis was convicted to only two months hard labour, and Payoo was acquitted.

Most Wendigo stories are from heavily forested regions with desperately long and harsh winters where the First Nations were hunter-gatherers wholly dependent on wild bounty for their survival. In years where game was scarce, starvation was a very real possibility. In light of that, there is a theory that the stories of the Wendigo have their origins in real events involving people, perhaps even entire tribes, who were forced to resort to cannibalism when food was scarce. Others suggest the tales are merely allegorical, intended to dissuade the eating of human flesh by warning that those who do will be tortured for all time as a soulless Wendigo. And then there are a few who suggest that, because many versions of Wendigo describe the fiend as a large humanoid of the woods, stories of the Wendigo are actually references to a carnivorous subspecies of Sasquatch that have turned to preying upon humans.

Whatever the truth, the Wendigo has gone from being a malevolent figure in First Nations myth to become a part of North American popular culture. Like Algernon Blackwood, August Derleth made the fiend the central figure of one of his tales of terror, "Ithaqua." The Wendigo has since been featured in countless books, movies (*Wendigo*, *Ravenous*, *The Last Winter*, *Pet Cemetery* and television shows.

These media representations are mere shadows of the true terror the Wendigo represented for First Nations Peoples. A reflection of the constant and very real fear of starvation, it stalked tribes like a silent predator, emerging from the cold northern skies to slay or seduce. After all, what could be more frightening than the nightmarish possibility that your loved ones could be lusting after your flesh?

# Chapter 23

# Sasquatch

~

North America's best-known monster, the legendary Sasquatch (Bigfoot) is a creature of incredible mystery. This giant ape-like creature stalks the wildest forests and mountains of the Pacific Northwest, lurking in regions rarely trod by human feet and only occasionally emerging from the shadowy depths of its woodland home to startle people.

Although there is as yet no scientific proof of its existence, First Nations traditions of the creature date back centuries. Most of the Indigenous Peoples across North America have stories in their oral traditions describing giant hairy figures, creatures that they absolutely believe to exist. The peoples are spread across the entire continent and represent all the linguistic groups of Indigenous languages. Every Indigenous linguistic group has its own name for Bigfoot, strongly suggesting the stories of these figures did not arise from a single location. In some cases these creatures were seen as brothers to humans or a type of nature spirit, but in many others these hairy giants were greatly feared.

In the last century and a half, many people of non-Indigenous descent have claimed to have seen Sasquatch as well. The descriptions they give are both of a terrifying monster and also something remarkably human-like, both in appearance and behaviour. All witnesses agree that Sasquatch usually stands at least 2.5 to 3 metres tall, is proportionately more massive than a human and weighs 300 to 1000 kilograms. It is bipedal and has dark skin covered in thick, coarse, black or auburn hair that covers the body from head to toe, save for its face, palms and soles, which are hairless. A Sasquatch's face is ape-like with a sloping brow, prominent eyebrow ridges, light-reflecting eyes (usually a nocturnal adaptation), broad flattened nose and lipless mouth. Its body is heavyset with a powerful, muscular chest and wide shoulders, very long arms and muscular legs that are said to be as thick as tree trunks. As its name suggests, Bigfoot has very large feet, leaving prints 30 to 60 centimetres long. Bigfoot walks with a long stride, leaning slightly forward, arms swinging and knees bent. Reports suggest the creature can run at speeds up to 65 kilometres per hour.

Many eyewitnesses report a persistent, musky odour that Sasquatch is said to give off. Researchers theorize that this scent serves as a method of marking territory or somehow aids in communication. Travellers in Bigfoot territory often report a sensation of being observed, as if something was monitoring their progress through the area. Whether Sasquatches are indeed watching or these reports are the products of overactive imaginations remains undetermined. The creatures are said to emit a number of distinctive vocalizations, including high-pitched whistles, animal-like screams and howls. Bigfoot are said to be omnivorous, eating berries, roots, rodents, larvae, carrion, fish, clams, deer and nuts.

Stories indicate that Sasquatches are sentient beings, and many claim they are only slightly less intelligent than humans, perhaps explaining in part how they are able to remain hidden and avoid detection despite the encroachment of civilization. In general they are peaceful creatures, steering clear of settlements and concealing themselves in the depths of mountain forests. A handful of tales, however, claim they will assault humans or even carry them off for unknown purposes.

One of the earliest accounts that hints at Sasquatch's violent tendencies dates back to March 1907. The steamer *Capilano* chugged into a First Nations village at Bishop Cove in British Columbia, and no sooner had the gangplank been extended than dozens of terrified villagers swarmed the vessel, desperately trying to force their way on board. When at last the people had been calmed down and convinced to speak, they explained that the community had been terrorized nightly by a towering man-ape, covered in long hair and with massive arms, that had come down to the beach at night to dig up clams. The creature would howl incessantly, sending shivers down the spines of the people cowering in their homes. They worried that soon its hunger would no longer be sated by clams and that the beast would then turn its attention upon them. They pleaded with the crew of the *Capilano* to be taken away.

A couple of decades later a sensational Bigfoot encounter took place, as told by British Columbia logger and prospector Albert Ostman. Ostman came forward in 1957 to recount an incident that he said had taken place in 1924. He'd remained silent for 30 years out of fear of ridicule. Ostman was prospecting at the head of Toba Inlet, opposite Vancouver Island, spending his nights in a primitive camp and sleeping in a sleeping bag under the stars. On the fifth night, a nocturnal prowler began tampering with his gear and rifling through his pack while he slept. Three nights later, something gathered Ostman up inside his sleeping bag and carried him away. After hours in the stifling darkness of his bag, he was dumped out to discover that he was the captive of a family of giant apelike creatures—an adult male and female, and two juveniles. They spoke in "chatter—some kind of talk I did not understand."

Though they were friendly, they clearly did not want him to escape from their canyon home. After a number of days in captivity, Ostman escaped by feeding the adult male a can of snuff, which caused him to choke, then firing a rifle shot to frighten the others. He then fled on foot and was so tormented by the experience he didn't speak of it to anyone for decades

Those who interviewed Ostman after he finally opened up about his kidnapping did not doubt his sincerity or sanity. Police magistrate A.M. Naismith interviewed him at length. "I cross-examined him and used every means to endeavor to find a flaw in either his personality or his story, but could find neither," he wrote in his official report. Over the years a number of scientists—including Smithsonian primatologist and paleoanthropologist John Napier—wrote that Ostman's account was convincing and sounded authentic.

There was another, less famous, abduction story from around the same period. Nootka tribesman Muchalat Harry was trapping on his native Vancouver Island in late autumn when, like Albert Ostman four years earlier, he was snatched from alongside the fire where he slept by a massive apelike

CANADIAN MONSTERS & MYTHICAL CREATURES

beast that carried him as effortlessly as a human carries a child. Harry was taken to a "sort of camp" occupied by half a dozen of these hairy monsters. The trapper was quite understandably initially fearful and was sure they were going to eat him, but they demonstrated no violence towards him whatsoever. After a day or so they seemed to lose interest in their captive and made no effort to stop him when he escaped. Upon arriving home, Harry's family was stunned by his appearance; his hair had turned pure white, and he was bedraggled and in poor health from stumbling through more than 70 kilometres of bush. Harry never returned for his traps, nor did he ever set foot in the woods again for the rest of his life—despite trapping being his livelihood.

One of the most famous Sasquatch cases ever, rivalling even the famous Albert Ostman kidnapping, took place in Ruby Creek, British Columbia. In September 1941, George and Annie Chapman and their three children inhabited a remote cabin in the area. On the afternoon in question, Annie, home with her children, noticed something approaching the cabin across an open field. At first she thought it might be a bear, but soon she was horrified to discover this was no animal. Instead, it was "a gigantic man covered with hair, not fur. The hair seemed to be about four inches [10 centimetres] long all over, and of a pale yellow-brown color." The creature stood over 2.5 metres tall, with a small head and no visible neck, long arms and a thick chest. Annie was terrified. She scooped up her children and left the cabin, fleeing downstream to a nearby village.

When George returned home that night, he found the cabin eerily empty, with signs that it had been hastily abandoned. Partially eaten food remained on the table, and a hamper of clothes had only half been hung on a line. George found an outbuilding ransacked, its door smashed in. Long brown hairs were stuck to the frame. A 200-litre barrel of salt fish had been dragged outside the shed and its contents scattered around the yard. George saw his family's tracks leading toward the river and was horrified to find the creature's huge footprints trailing after them. To his relief, he later found his family safe and sound, sheltered in the nearby village. But the ordeal wasn't over quite yet. After returning to their cabin, the Chapmans would wake every morning to find fresh giant-sized footprints in the yard, sometimes just metres from the cabin's flimsy walls. It was a week filled with anxiety and anticipation, which only lifted after the Sasquatch seemingly lost interest in the family and no longer came around.

In October 1955, William Roe encountered a Sasquatch while hunting near Tête Jaune Cache, a small town in British Columbia. He spotted the creature from a distance and, like Annie Chapman, initially mistook it for a bear. Roe realized his error when the "bear" stood up and began walking on two legs. According to his sworn affidavit:

> [M]y *first impression was of a huge man, about six feet* [2 metres] *tall, almost three feet* [1 metre] *wide, and probably weighing somewhere near 300 pounds* [150 kilograms]. *It was covered from head to foot with dark brown silver-tipped hair. But as it came closer I saw by its breasts that it was female.*
>
> *And yet, its torso was not curved like a female's. Its broad frame was straight from shoulder to hip. Its arms were much thicker than a man's arms, and longer, reaching almost to its knees. Its feet were broader proportionately than a man's, about five inches*

*[12 centimetres] wide at the front and tapering to*
*much thinner heels. When it walked it placed the heel*
*of its foot down first, and I could see the grey-brown*
*skin or hide on the soles of its feet.*

The creature evidently caught Roe's scent because it
stopped suddenly in its tracks and turned to look directly at
him through an opening in the brush. The creature then
turned and walked rapidly away, turning once or twice to
gaze back at him. Roe raised his rifle to shoot, aware that if he
killed the creature it would be of immense scientific interest,
but he couldn't bring himself to squeeze the trigger. "Although
I have called the creature 'it,' I felt now that it was a human
being and I knew I would never forgive myself if I killed it," he
explained.

Although these stories are dramatic and even frightening,
Bigfoot didn't gain widespread recognition until 1958 after an
incident in California. A mysterious nighttime visitor plagued
a road construction crew, disturbing their camp. It carried
a 200-litre oil drum 50 metres from the construction site and
tossed it into a gorge, threw an 45-centimetre culvert pipe
weighing more than 100 kilograms down another slope, and
rolled a 115-kilogram earthmover's tire nearly a kilometre from
the work site before pitching it into a deep ravine. The culprit
was never seen but left behind a number of enormous footprints.
Jerry Crew, a bulldozer operator, called a friend to take plaster
casts of the footprints. Pictures of theses casts were published in
a local newspaper, the *Humboldt Times,* on October 5, along
with the word "Bigfoot"—the first time this name had ever
been lent to Sasquatch. Soon major media outlets were reporting the story, and Bigfoot became a phenomenon.

A decade later, interest in Bigfoot reached new heights
after Roger Patterson filmed what is purportedly a Bigfoot at

Bluff Creek, California, on October 20, 1967. Patterson was a former rodeo rider who had become fascinated with Bigfoot and wrote a book entitled, *Do Abominable Snowmen of Canada Really Exist*. He set out to make a documentary on Bigfoot, and it was while shooting background footage that he filmed the 952 frames that would make him famous.

Rancher Bob Gimlin accompanied Patterson to Bluff Creek. The two men spotted a massive, hairy hominid crouched in the middle of a creek. It must have been startled by the horses they were riding, because the creature suddenly stood up to a height Patterson estimated was over 2.5 metres and then briskly walked towards the wood. Patterson had the presence of mind to grab his 16mm handheld Kodak movie camera and begin rolling. The creature walked away into the forest, turning its head once toward the camera before disappearing. Patterson and Gimlin tracked it for 5 kilometres but lost the trail in the heavy undergrowth. The Patterson film, although short and shaky, clearly revealed a massive ape-like beast with a conical head, powerful muscles, pendulous breasts and dark brown hair. In addition, the men made casts of a series of 10 footprints measuring 35 centimetres long and 15 centimetres wide.

In the half century since, Bigfoot has entered the public imagination like few monsters have, becoming the subject of countless books, magazine articles, documentaries and even several feature films. And, of course, thousands of people have claimed that they've seen these hairy hominids.

The question is, what weight do eyewitness accounts carry with mainstream science? In truth very little because, as any police officer will tell you, witness testimony is remarkably unreliable. Some people lie outright. Others will make mistakes, particularly under stress—such as when encountering

an unknown creature in the wild—or when in unfamiliar surroundings, as the wilderness certainly is for the vast majority of us. Undoubtedly some Bigfoot encounters are a case of misidentification of recognized species wildlife at distance. Two animals that might easily be mistaken for a bipedal hominid are bears or wolverines, both of which are known to stand on two legs for brief periods. As a result, Bigfoot skeptics are right to suggest that eyewitness testimony alone isn't enough to prove the existence of a species presently unrecognized by science. At the same time, skeptics surely cannot discount all accounts as being lies or misidentification.

What's needed to satisfy the scientific community is proof. Evidence, if not actual proof, of Sasquatches is surprisingly abundant for a creature that science would have you believe doesn't exist. The most common signs of a Sasquatch, as we all know, are the familiar giant footprints that have been found all over the Pacific Northwest. Not only are the tracks

SASQUATCH

much larger than a human's foot, measuring 30 to 50 centimetres long and proportionately wide, but the imprints sink several inches into the soil, a testament to the creature's great weight (estimated to be as great as 900 kilograms). Literally hundreds of Bigfoot casts have surfaced over the past half-century, and though some are assuredly faked—some cleverly so—one cannot discount all of them. Some of the footprints are so detailed that they even exhibit distinctive forensic features, such as, dermatoglyphs (fingerprints) and pressure cracks, which are nearly impossible to fake and therefore indicate to researchers that the footprints are real.

The sheer number of casts made over the years does lend considerable weight to the possibility that Sasquatch does indeed exist. "The possibility of a hoax to explain all the casts," John Napier once noted in reference to the tracks, "is even more remote than that of the animal existing." He noted that a vast conspiracy would have to exist, with participants venturing into some of Canada's most remote areas, for all the tracks to be fake.

A remarkable set of casts was made near Bossburg, in northern Washington State, in 1969 by Bigfoot researcher Ivan Marx. Although some in the Bigfoot research community consider Marx a hoaxer and a "yarn-spinner," no one can say that the so-called Bossburg Prints were not cause for excitement. The creature's left foot measured 43 centimetres long, 15 centimetres across the ball and 12 centimetres across the heel. The right foot, however, showed signs of deformity. It measured a full 3 centimetres less in both length and width.

John Napier, a British primatologist and paleoanthropologist, and generally a harsh critic of the work of most Bigfoot researchers and their so-called "evidence," was truly impressed by the Bossburg Prints. In his book, *Bigfoot: The Yeti and Sasquatch in Myth and Reality*, he writes of the casts:

*Apart from satisfying the criteria established for modern human-type walking, the Bossburg prints have, to my way of thinking, an even greater claim to authenticity. The right foot of the Bossburg Sasquatch is a club-foot, a not uncommon abnormality...the forepart of the foot is twisted inwards, the third toe has been squeezed out of normal alignment, and possibly there has been a dislocation of the bones on the outer border (but this last feature may be due to an imperfection in the casting technique). Clubfoot usually occurs as a congenital abnormality, but it may also develop as the result of severe injury, or of damage to the nerves controlling the muscle of the foot. To me the deformity strongly suggests that injury during life was responsible...I conclude that the deformity was the result of a crushing injury to the foot during early childhood. It is very difficult to conceive of a hoaxer so subtle, so knowledgeable—and so sick—who would deliberately fake a footprint of this nature. I suppose it is possible, but it is so unlikely that I am prepared to discount it.*

Sadly, Marx's later behaviour of faked films and a host of other improbable evidence have overshadowed the importance of the Bossburg Prints. The question one has to ask is, was Marx a hoaxer from the beginning, or were the Bossburg Prints real and the subsequent "evidence" simply a man's desperate attempt to remain relevant and in the spotlight.

Perhaps the most exciting casts to emerge in recent years were made from prints found at Mill Creek in Oregon's Blue Mountains in 1993. What these casts revealed threw the Bigfoot research community into elation. Clearly evident in the casts were dermal ridges, which create the fingerprint and footprints unique to individuals. These are found only on the palms and soles of primates and are almost impossible to accurately fake.

Dozens of experts—ranging from police fingerprint experts to anthropologists, pathologists and zoologists—who studied the casts agree that the detailed anatomy has all the characteristics and appearance of being made by a primate. The size of the casts, around 45 centimetres long, and their shape and morphology rule out any known primate, including humans. Even representatives of the Smithsonian Institution, an organization that is always the harshest critic of cryptozoology, agrees that the cast was made by a primate. Fingerprint experts John Berry and Stephen Haylock examined the casts and opined that "these casts appear to represent the foot of a highly unusual creature, flatfooted in the extreme...." They concluded that if the cast was faked, the hoaxer deserved the Lewis Minshall Award, which is issued annually by the Fingerprint Society to members who make outstanding contributions in the field.

Taken together, the uniform morphology of the tracks, including small details, and their wide distribution over vast and remote geographic areas suggests authenticity in at least some of the hundreds put forward to this date. Tantalizing finds continue to the present day, but so, too, does the fierce debate over the authenticity of Bigfoot casts.

Visible evidence also includes countless mats of hair caught on branches and undergrowth over the decades, at or near the scenes of Bigfoot sightings. Sadly, these generally turn out to be from other animals, or even humans. Some, however, have yielded curious results under analysis. The first sample to undergo such testing was from Bluff Creek in 1958. Dr. F. Martin Duncan, head of the London Zoo's extensive animal hair collection, examined the strands and reported that, in his expert opinion, they "did not match any known North American mammal, but that they would be from an unknown and very large primate."

Science has come a long way in the past 60 years, yet on occasion, hair samples continue to confound scientists. As a case in point, in 1993 Dr. Sterling Bunnell, a member of the California Academy of Sciences, studied hair samples collected from northern California and reported that the animal they came from was "clearly related to the human-chimpanzee-gorilla group, but is distinguishable from each of these." He noted that the specimen hairs were "remarkable in the extremely fine and diffuse pigmentation (other species show dark melanin clumps and medullary streaks) and the absence of observable medullary structure." In other worlds, the hairs came from something closely related to humans and the known great apes, yet distinct from these species. Dr. Bunnell was confounded by what he had studied. This all being said, until we have a hair tested for DNA and that comes back anomalous, such opinions are just that—opinions and conjecture, albeit based on professional expertise.

Multiple samples of purported Bigfoot feces have been collected over the years as well, but as with hair, most come back belonging to a common animal. Thus far, this line of evidence has been unfruitful and is unlikely ever to be useful because scat doesn't include DNA or other defining character-istics that could be considered proof of existence. And what about bones—why have no Bigfoot bones ever been found? Researchers will reply—with some justification—that the remoteness of Bigfoot habitat makes this relatively unlikely. When was the last time a hiker came across a grizzly skele-ton? Even biologists will agree that such a find is extremely rare, as nature is extremely efficient in recycling itself. This admission makes it even less likely that the deceased remains of a very rare, perhaps even endangered mystery beast would be happened upon. And what if, as some speculate, Sasquatches are intelligent and social enough to bury their dead? In such a case, finding skeletal remains would be most improbable.

Many researchers will point to broken tree branches at heights of 2 or 3 metres the ground, or even entire trees snapped in half or uprooted, as evidence of Bigfoot's existence. Linking Sasquatch to such phenomenon is actually nothing new, as many traditional First Nations stories tell of the creatures doing similar things. In fact, some peoples have names for Bigfoot that can be translated as "stick Indians" for the manner in which they snap trees and break branches. Because many things can cause such damage, researchers focus on limbs above the reach of bears or humans. Dr. Wolf-Henrich Fahrenbach looks for a specific type of breakage when looking for evidence of Bigfoot: green limbs, 5 or 10 centimetres thick, where "damage does indeed appear to be related to the twisting by an animal with superhuman strength combined with a powerful and flexible grip which twists the stem, splintering it internally, without shredding or removing the bark." Skeptics will say such damage can be caused by rot, the passage of large animals like bear or moose, wind or snow load or even human hoax.

The Patterson Tape is still considered some of the most compelling Bigfoot evidence we have. Patterson and Gimlin went to their graves sticking to their story, but it remains controversial. On the other hand, some special effects film people claim it is common knowledge in Hollywood that the filmed Bigfoot was a man in a suit designed by a special effects artist. Indeed, some pinpoint John Chambers, best known as the famed makeup artist behind the *Planet of the Apes* films, as the individual responsible even though he always denied any involvement and had only manufactured ape-man masks, not suits, for the movies. Also, when Bigfoot researcher John Green contacted experts at the Disney Studios for their opinion as to whether the techniques for creating the Patterson film were available in 1967, the experts told him that they could not have duplicated it at the time even though Disney was at the forefront of special effects in the 1960s.

The film has undergone considerable forensic examination over the years by experts in a number of fields. Under close scrutiny, a number of aspects emerge that lead some scientists to endorse it as genuine. The movement of the creature's muscles beneath its hair strongly argues against a hoax. In addition, they point out that a human wearing a suit could not achieve the unusual striding gait and lengthy strides performed by the creature. The swinging of the creature's arms is decidedly un-human, and the skin seems consistent with that of a living creature rather than a suit. Finally, the Bigfoot of the Patterson Film has pendulous breasts, indicative of a female. Most argue that it's unlikely a hoaxer would think to make the specimen a female.

Skeptics often ask why there is no archeological evidence of Sasquatch if the creature exists. Even for recognized prehistoric primates, fossil records are few and far between. With *Gigantopithecus*, for example, only four jaws and about a thousand teeth have been found in all of Asia. It's interesting to note that we have no fossils for gorillas or gorilla ancestors, yet as we know, these animals most assuredly exist. Worse still for the likelihood of finding Sasquatch remains, as many paleontologists will point out, is the fact that fossils are actually rarer in North America than other parts of the world because the glaciers that covered large parts of the continent long go destroyed such evidence.

Simply put, though, the only evidence that would satisfy the scientific community and most of the world at large is DNA or the body of a dead Sasquatch.

So let's assume for a moment that Sasquatch does in fact exist. What exactly is it? As far as the identity of the species goes, the favourite contender seems to the huge, prehistoric ape-like creature called *Gigantopithecus* that formerly lived in Asia but officially died out around somewhere between 300,000 and 100,000 years ago. *Gigantopithecus blacki*, which lived in southern China and Vietnam, was the largest known primate to ever live, standing 3 metres tall and weighing as much as 600 kilograms. Interestingly, they were contemporary with anatomically modern humans. There was also a smaller member of the family, *Gigantopithecus giganteus*, which, despite its name, was probably closer to half the size of *G. blacki*. We don't know much about the appearance of these prehistoric apes because of the fragmentary nature of their fossil remains; thus far, only jaws and teeth have been found. Based on dimensions alone, however, *Gigantopithecus* seems eerily reminiscent of eyewitness accounts of Bigfoot.

Cryptozoologists will further point out that no satisfactory explanation for *Gigantopithecus'* extinction has so far been put forward. It has been postulated that climate change was the cause of their demise, that forests gave way to grasslands and thereby deprived the species of its primary food supply. This is just a theory; however, with no real foundation upon which to rest. Simply put, we don't know why—and some would argue, even if—*Gigantopithecus* went extinct.

The fact that *Gigantopithecus* was native to Asia doesn't pose a problem for those arguing it is the creature behind the

Bigfoot myth. They will point out that while the mega-primate existed, Asia was linked by a land bridge to Alaska. Many other animal species crossed the bridge and established themselves in what became the New World, so why not *Gigantopithecus* as well? If *Gigantopithecus* did indeed make this migration, and furthermore if a surviving population has persisted here right up to the present day while successfully eluding scientific detection, these creatures could explain reports of Bigfoot.

While *Gigantopithecus* is the forerunner, there are other candidates for Bigfoot's identity. Others have suggested Sasquatch might be a bipedal hominid named *Paranthropus robustus* that emerged about 2.7 million years ago. Researcher and cryptozoologist Gordon Strasenburgh originally put forward the idea in 1971. This species was well-muscled with a broad, gorilla-like chest and had a brain about 40 percent the size of modern human's, so that while it probably did not have language or make fire, it seems to have made tools. There's one problem with this theory: *Paranthropus* stood only 1.3 to 1.4 metres tall, far smaller than any reported Bigfoot. Strasenburgh argues that *Paranthropus* may have evolved over the course of two million years.

Cryptozoologist Loren Coleman has his own theory: Bigfoot might be surviving examples of *Meganthropus*, a little-known hominid genus, possibly a *Homo erectus* subspecies or even a Southeast Asian representation of Australopithecines, whose remains were found in Java in 1939 and 1941. Some have even suggested the Sasquatch might be descended from Neandertals or an entirely new and previously undocumented hominid. Any of these various scenarios are amazing in terms of their potential implications.

The more one digs into Bigfoot lore, the more questions emerge. Perhaps this is why the cryptid has become so ingrained in our popular culture and public consciousness. A folklorist might suggest our fascination with Sasquatch stems from a subconscious need to believe in some large-than-life creature, or perhaps some underlying fear of the unknown dangers that might lurk in the wilderness. Whatever the truth may be, the possibility that a large primate stalks the forested mountains of the Pacific Northwest continues to fascinate and intrigue.

Scientists tell us Bigfoot doesn't exist zoologists offer a host of reasons why they cannot exist, and historians assure us they are nothing more than folklore. But the weight of evidence—eyewitness accounts, footprints, unusual hairs and other anomalies—suggests they are living entities. I want to believe in Sasquatch, and I think it's highly plausible that the vast wildernesses, deep forests and massive ranges of the Pacific Northwest could be home to a species not yet identified by science. Still, I admit the burden of proof lies with the researchers trying to prove Bigfoot's existence.

The elusive Sasquatch continues to earn its mysterious reputation.

# Appendix

# Additional Canadian Monsters

~

Carnivorous mice. Cougars with long, prehensile tails. Moose that dine on human flesh. Canada has far more strange and even sinister monsters than could possibly comfortably fit in any book. Here, in capsule form, is a brief look at some more monsters from Canadian myth and legend.

## Angeoa

The elusive Angeoa is the terror of Dubawnt Lake in Nunavut. The Inuit who dwell near the lake warn travellers of the monstrosity that hunts within and around the water, but few have actually seen the dread beast up close. Fewer still have survived an attack by this ravenous freshwater monster— it snatches up victims from land and shore with incredible reach and lightning speed, dragging its hapless prey into the lake, where it either drowns its victim or tears its prey apart with its jagged teeth.

Those who have seen the monster and lived to tell of it describe a colossal, arching creature measuring 10 or 12 metres in length, its hide as black as a starless night's sky. The Angeoa has an enormous back fin, short side fins, a split tail and a maw filled with sharp teeth.

An Inuit man told Canadian author Farley Mowat in the 1940s that his father had encountered the Angeoa at the end of the 19th century. The beast had overturned his kayak with its bulk and then turned its blood-rage upon the man's hunting companion. In the flash of a mere second or two—a fin suddenly breaking the surface, followed by a bite that turned the frigid waters red—the companion was killed and pulled beneath the water's surface.

What is the Angeoa? Many are too scared to even ask the question. But some cryptozoologists say descriptions sound like a killer whale (or orca), hypothesizing that a population somehow became trapped in the freshwater lake, perhaps thousands of years ago, and has endured there ever since.

## Angont

It has dwelled beneath Lake Huron for centuries, perhaps even since time began, an elemental thing of malice and eternal hunger. Those who take to the waters of this Great Lake do so at their own peril, for some invariably end up in the waiting jaws of the Angont. On moonless nights, it is said, the beast can be seen rising to the surface, as pale as a ghost, a spectre given physical form.

The Angont, also known as the Oniare ("snake") in the tongue of the Mohawk people, resides primarily in Lake

Huron, but some claim to have seen it venturing up rivers that feed this massive lake. There have even been tales of the Angont as far away as Lake Michigan. This massive, snake-like creature has bull-like horns atop its head. A mouth full of jagged teeth hint at its predatory nature, and prominent fangs drip with noxious venom. The snakeskin hide is often described as being a deathly white, though other times the color can be as black as a moonless night. The creature's breath is said to be so poisonous that a mere whiff will kill even the strongest bear.

Iroquois lore makes it clear the Angont lurks beneath the waves, prowling for unwary victims. It capsizes canoes, throwing the passengers into the water where they become easy prey for its gaping maw. In some traditions, the Angont will spare travelers who make offerings to it, and there are dark tales of Iroquois tribes drowning people as a sacrifice to appease her hunger and ensure safe travels. Traditional enemies made claims that the Iroquois were somehow given the gift of poison by the Angont, but that may simply be the whispered tales of people who feared the might of the "Iroquois Confederacy."

The Angont isn't merely First Nations myth. A serpentine monster has been seen in Georgian Bay, especially around Wasaga Beach, numerous times in recent memory.

## Ashuaps

The legendary Ashuaps is said to lurk beneath the waters of Québec's Lac St. Jean. It's a creature shrouded in mystery. Indeed, some First Nations Peoples who dwell in the region believe that to speak of the dark creature is to invite death. Legends speak of the carnage Ashuaps has caused when roused.

Lac St. Jean is a large lake that spans 659 square kilometres and has a depth of nearly 70 metres at its deepest point, plenty big enough to hide terrible beasts of monstrous proportions. The First Nations Peoples who lived in the area had long known of the creature and believed it was best to avoid it. They claimed the beast's lair was on, or under, Grass Snake Island.

Even though there had been sightings since ancient times, it wasn't until the 1950s that the monster appeared in print and earned its name—Ashuaps, from the Ashuapmouchouan River, which flows into Lac St. Jean. Some sightings involved little more than a large, dark body with humps moving through the water out in the distance. Others, however, were more detailed and painted a vivid picture of a true monster. A massive saurian creature measuring between 10 and 35 metres in length, it sports a triangular "dinosaur-like" head that stretches forth from a long, snaking neck. Long spines run down its back and into a long, whip-like tail. Its leathery hide is deep blue or black in color.

The two most notable encounters with Ashuaps took place on the same fateful day in 1978. In the first, Marcel Tardif and his wife watched from the shoreline as a black animal, 17 and 20 metres long, appeared in the water off Scott Point. The creature rose up out of the water and then submerged again, repeating this behaviour several times before slipping beneath the water and disappearing.

Late in the afternoon that same day, Michel Verreault, his wife and their daughter were canoeing in Lac St. Jean, blissfully unaware that something lurked below. Something that had taken an unusual interest in them. Without warning, something huge slammed into the bottom of the Verreault's canoe, flipping it over and violently throwing the family into the lake. While treading water, they saw a long, black serpentine creature swimming in a wide circle around them, just below the surface. Naturally terrified, they hurriedly righted the canoe, piled back in and raced for shore.

Sightings of Ashuaps continued well into the 1980s but inexplicably began to slow in the 1990s. This has led some to surmise the creature may have died or left the lake through one of the rivers that flow into it, only returning on occasion. Could it now be safe to go back into the waters of Lac St. Jean?

## Atchen

The Atchen (also spelled Atcen) are violent, bloodthirsty cannibal giants of eastern Canada. Standing at least 3.5 metres tall, they are stooped and misshapen with dim eyes that reveal an even dimmer intellect.

The First Nations Peoples of north-central Québec and Nova Scotia feared the dreadful Atchen. They told stories of Atchen—stories of brutality and savagery, cannibalism and torture. Those who survived such encounters knew these tales were tame compared to the truth. While blessedly rare, Atchen would occasionally emerge from the shadows of the deepest, darkest forests to cull humans and descend upon tribes in a bloodlust of violence. Those who died quickly at the hands of these ill-tempered brutes were the lucky ones. Others endured unspeakable torture and humiliation before the death they prayed for finally ended their suffering. Even then, their one final defilement awaited: The Atchen would cut off the victim's hands and feet before devouring them. Without hands or feet, the spirit was helpless in the afterlife.

Atchen reside in dismal, dreary, ugly places far from the sight of man—deep swamps, rugged and windswept hills, and forests so thick the floor has never felt the sun's touch. Even today such places are best avoided…just in case.

## Gougou

In 1603, Mi'kmaq guides warned Samuel de Champlain to avoid the Isle of Miscou in Chaleur Bay, on the south side of the Gulf of St. Lawrence. To venture near was to court disaster, or death. Champlain wrote that the Mi'kmaq told him there was a frightful monster, the Gougou, which was magically bound to this island and all the waters around it. And frightful it truly was.

The Gougou was a cruelly beautiful woman but, as Champlain writes, "most hideous, and of such size that according to them the tops of the masts of our vessel would not reach its waist." When a vessel approaches her island, the skies darken and rumble, and then there is a strange and sudden surging of the sea as the Gougou rises from the depths to attack her human prey. Some of her victims she eats right away, such is her hunger, but others she puts in a massive pocket to be consumed at a later date. These pockets, Champlain recorded, "are so large that she could have put our vessel into it."

At first, as an educated and worldly man who had seen much in his travels, Champlain did not believe the stories his Indigenous guides had told him about the Gougou. Even when they desperately beseeched him not to send one of his vessels near the Isle of Miscou, he thought it little more than superstition. That soon changed.

Captain Prevert, commander of one of the ships Champlain had dispatched into the dreaded realm of the Gougou, returned with a terrifying story. While the mariner Prevert insisted he had not actually seen the Gougou, he and his entire crew heard the creature "hissing" when he passed near her lair, as if the giantess was seething with anger and bubbling over with nearly uncontrollable hunger. Champlain, taking note of his commander's concern and of the Mi'kmaq's obvious fear of the Gougou, made a note to always make a wide berth around the island in the future to remain out of reach of the vicious beast.

## Halifax Alligator Monster

Citizens of London, England, in the summer of 1752 were excited to hear reports of the sea-monster that was caught and brought ashore in the colonial town of "Hallifax" in Nova Scotia. According to the story in *London Magazine*, fishermen captured the beast in their nets and proudly displayed it for all to see when they returned to port on May 28 after a month at sea. The creature was a terror to behold:

> ...a sea monster, a female of the kind, whose body was about the bigness of that of a large ox, and something resembling one, covered with short hair, of brownish colour; the skin near one inch and a half thick, very loose and rough; the neck thick and short, resembling that of a bull; the head small in proportion to the body, and very like an alligator; in the upper jaws were two teeth of about nine or ten inches long, and crooked downwards; the legs were very short and thick, ending with fins and claws, like those of a sea-turtle; the flesh and inwards have been opened, and resemble those of an ox or horse.

What the heck was this thing? It might sound like a sea lion, though sea lions are not native to Canada's Atlantic coast. If not for the predatory-sounding teeth and the fact they are a tropical species that travel no farther north than the rivers and mangrove swamps of Florida, you might be tempted to say it was a manatee. But what if it was some sort of previously unidentified form of aquatic life, perhaps a rare and now extinct form of sea lion, or maybe something even more terrible? Sadly, no remains of the slain beast were kept, so we will never know.

## Hugag

The Hugag is one of the oddest creatures said to inhabit the North American wilderness, ranging from as far north as Hudson Bay to Wisconsin and Minnesota in the south. This beast resembles a moose, and is comparable in size, standing 2 metres at the shoulder and weighing as much as 800 kilograms. The resemblance is only superficial; however, as the Hugag has a number of defining—and decidedly unusual—characteristics. It has a long tail, much like that of a horse; four toes per foot instead of hooves; a completely bald, leathery head and neck; corrugated, floppy ears; shaggy fur; and legs without joints, which means it walks awkwardly.

The most distinctive feature, however, is an upper lip that droops to such an extent that it hangs near the ground. This lip is used to scrape needles and twigs off pine trees. The Hugag eats some of these needles and covers itself with others—the needles are held in place by pine sap, which oozes from the pores in the Hugag's hide.

The Hugag has an abundance of stamina. It can reportedly walk all day long, browsing on twigs and stripping bark off trees, before finally tiring at nightfall. Because its legs have no joints, the Hugag cannot lie down to sleep. Instead, it leans wearily against a tree. First Nations Peoples had an ingenious way of hunting these beasts. They would notch trees so that the trees were nearly ready to fall. When a Hugag tired and leaned against it, both the tree and the animal would crash to the ground, rendering the animal helpless and easy for the hunter to kill.

## Kisihohkew

Moose represented an important food source for the Ojibwe. First Nations hunters would stalk these massive deer through dense forests, armed only with bow and arrow and spear. But did moose occasionally stalk the hunters in turn? The Cree believed so. The Kisihohkew, a species of carnivorous moose, preyed only upon humans. Most accounts say the Kisihohkew was virtually indistinguishable from a normal moose, save for the razor-sharp teeth that fill its mouth. A few, however, suggest the monster had some wolf-like features that help set it apart, though by the time you recognized the difference, you were likely facing your final moments.

Even an ordinary moose is a terrifyingly powerful animal when roused. Standing as tall as a horse, they are 450 kilograms of pure muscle with a massive rack of antlers atop a sturdy head and are capable of running 55 kilometres per hour. Now add flesh-ripping teeth and bone crushing jaw muscles— understandably, the Ojibwe greatly feared the Kishihohkew.

## Lake Erie Monster

The startling appearances of the Lake Erie Monster litter dozens of campfire tales and maritime yarns. First Nations legends say the creature would creep onto shore to steal children, but this monster isn't confined to ancient myth. There have been dozens of reputable sightings over the course of the past two centuries.

The first recorded sighting occurred in 1793 when a group of men came ashore on Middle Bass Island from the sloop *Felicity* to hunt ducks. Along the water's edge, a man fired at some ducks paddling in a marshy area. The roar of the musket startled something that had been resting unseen in the reeds: a 5-metre long serpent. The beast burst from the underbrush and chased after the man as he fled in terror.

Crewmen aboard the schooner *General Scott* reported another monster serpent a century later, on July 3, 1880. As the lake's surface was nearly flat, the crew was able to observe the serpent for more than a minute and get a good look at it. It was about 12 metres long, had a neck 30 centimetres in diameter and had skin that was almost black.

On the evening of May 5, 1896, four people lounging at Crystal Beach near Fort Erie sighted the serpent again. At first they thought the commotion was caused by a school of fish, but it soon became apparent it was in fact a single large creature. For 45 minutes, they watched it swim back and forth through the surf, presumably hunting for prey. Measuring about 12 metres long, the serpent had a head that looked like a dog's and a pointed tail.

The following year a group of Detroit businessmen came face-to-face with the monster offshore near Sarnia. They were fishing a few miles offshore in about 50 metres of water when suddenly a "black mass, a swiftly moving ribbon-shaped monster, dashed to the surface." Startled, one of the fishermen began firing on the monster with a revolver and must have wounded it because the water was soon crimson with blood. The creature was at least 25 metres, was as flexible as a snake, and had a double row of fins and long whiskers on its face. The injured serpent dove to escape and wasn't seen again.

Either the creature survived or there is more than one of these colossal beasts because one was sighted offshore near Sarnia again in 1938, when six fishermen were forced to run their boat ashore because of the assault of an undulating, 10-metre serpent with a menacing tail that swished back and forth.

There was a flurry of sightings in 1993. One family of four saw the creature just offshore near Lowbanks, Ontario. It was moving rapidly through the water and was said to be 10 metres long. Around the same time, two fishermen on separate occasions saw the monster. And then there was the episode when a man walking his dog along the shore startled a coiled snake of epic proportions. It dove into the lake and was gone before the man really had a chance to process what he was seeing.

The Lake Erie Monster has been a part of local lore for so long and has been seen by so many people that a group of Huron, Ohio, businessmen offered a reward of $100,000 to anyone who could prove the monster existed. So far, no one has been able to claim the reward.

## Loup Garou

For seventeen horrifying months in 1766 and 1767 the area around Québec City was terrorized by a Loup Garou, the French-Canadian werewolf. Doors were barred at night, men rarely left home unarmed, and every sound in the night was imagined to be a blood-raged beast ready to pounce.

The panic began in July 1766 when the *Québec Gazette* reported that a "ware wolf" was wandering around in the guise of a beggar. He would lull people into a false sense of security with this unassuming appearance before transforming into a man-wolf and ripping apart his unsuspecting victims. "The beast," the newspaper continued, "is said to be as dangerous as that which appear'd last year in the Country of Gevaudan [referring to a werewolf that killed more than a dozen people in Gevaudan, now Auverne, France, from 1764 and 1767]; wherefore it is recommended to the Public to be as cautious of him as it would be of a ravenous wolf."

There was a follow-up story on December 11 of the following year, making it clear the Loup Garou was still about. According to the article, the "Ware-wolfe" that was roaming the province had "done great Destruction in the District of Quebec [City]." Mobs had attacked the beast and apparently injured it so severely that for a time it was thought to have been slain, but the Loup Garou had merely lain low while licking its wounds. By the end of 1767, it was clear the beast was stalking the province again. "This Beast is not entirely destroyed," the paper reported, "but begins again to show itself, more furious than ever, and makes terrible Hovock [sic] wherever he goes."

Such a rampage was hardly unheard of. Loup Garou attacks were especially common in France from the 12th through the 17th century. Lycanthropy is a form of disease that spread almost unhindered through the populace. It spread by one of two methods: A person was bitten by a Loup Garou or was the offspring of one and was cursed to become a werewolf in turn, changing shape uncontrollably when a full moon rose. A Loup Garou might live undetected for decades by hiding amidst the masses of humanity, but by the 1600s things were getting hot in France as soldiers hunted wolves and werewolves to the point of extinction. Legend has it that a number of Loup Garou fled to New France to escape persecution, and there, in the sparsely settled and heavily forested colony, prospered. They preyed on livestock, women and children, and the occasional lone male.

The Loup Garou has the same weaknesses as the standard werewolf of popular fiction and film, notably wolfsbane and silver weapons. There are notable differences, however. Québecois lore holds that, in addition to being compelled to transform into a wolf or wolf-man hybrid upon the arrival of a full moon, a Loup Garou can change at will and maintains its human intellect throughout its period as a monster. As a result, it is a far more insidious creature than the run-of-the-mill werewolf.

The Loup Garou remains a staple of Québecois lore today. Is this because it makes for a thrilling yarn, or is it because the Loup Garou is still out there, skulking in the shadows, prowling through the woods, searching for vulnerable victims?

## Mishepishu

The Ojibwe rightfully feared the creature they called Mishepishu (which translates as "great lynx"). Other First Nations Peoples referred to it as the Water Cougar. But whatever name it went by, the Mishepishu was a blight upon whatever land it chose to despoil.

Details of the creature's appearance vary from culture to culture, but it is generally described as being a cross between a feline (such as a cougar or lynx) and a dragon. Its serpent-like body is covered in scales and stretches as much as 7 metres long, with saw-tooth-like growths running down its back and into a prehensile tail made of copper. The creature has a large, cat-like head topped with either horns or antlers, and with a mouthful of fangs that can effortlessly shred flesh and crush bone. Its roar is the sound of a raging storm, and its hiss is that of rushing rapids. Some sources say it can change shape from its natural serpentine form to a massive lynx with horns or a human being, the better to infiltrate villages.

Mishepishu is among the most dangerous beasts to be found around the Great Lakes. Its sleek build and stealthy manner allow it to stalk victims like the deftest woodland hunter, preying predominantly on humans and in particular their children. Those slain are dragged back to its lair for later consumption.

Although the vile creature is called the Great Lynx and stalks the forests for prey, it actually lives in aquatic lairs in the deepest waters of lakes and rivers. A particularly feared Mishepishu has laid claim to Michipicoten Island on Lake Superior, making the island taboo to First Nations Peoples. Mishepishu is believed to be the master of all water creatures, including snakes. It creates storms that swamp or upend canoes and causes people to drown, then drags their bloated bellies below the water. To ensure safe passage across a large lake, would-be travellers need to placate Mishepishu with gifts.

## Mussie

Is Mussie a figment of whimsical fantasy, or is she a real cryptid awaiting discovery? It depends on who you ask. According to some, the whole thing is a joke, made apparent by a description that sounds like something out of Wonderland—three eyes, three ears, one big fin halfway down its back, two legs, a single big tooth in its mouth, silver-green coloration and a body that stretches 8 metres long. Others will say that naysayers concocted this outlandish description to make fun of those who claim to have spotted an unknown creature in Muskrat Lake. Certainly, there's enough evidence to suggest the latter is the case.

The first known sighting of Mussie emerged in 1916, and in the century since, at least a dozen individuals have come forward with claims of having seen a strange beast swimming in the lake. One or two people have even seen it shuffling about awkwardly on the shoreline. Although accounts differ in specific details of Mussie's anatomy and behaviour, in general, most agree it measures 3 to 7 metres long, is dark in coloration, has a dog-like head, and swims up and down like a seal. A few, however, claim the creature actually looks like a plesiosaur in the mould of the Loch Ness Monster.

Author Michael Bradley devoted a whole book—*More Than a Myth: The Search for the Monster of the Muskrat Lake* (1989)—to the cryptid. During the course of writing the book, Bradley spent countless hours patrolling the lake in a specially designed boat equipped with sonar in an attempt to locate the monster. Incredibly, he claims to have done so. Near the mouth of the Snake River, he spotted what looked to be a pair of 3-metre-long marine mammals that looked reminiscent of large seals. Not long after, a woman named Dana Rogers captured a similar-looking creature on film.

With underwater trenches extending some 60 metres deep, it's certainly possible something dwells within the depths of Muskrat Lake. It's also possible that seals might have migrated up the St. Lawrence and its watershed to establish a colony in the lake. Or, the lake monster might all be a flight of fancy created by some locals in years past and perpetuated today to bring in tourism dollars. Muskrat Lake, it seems, gives up its secrets reluctantly.

## Nani-Bajou

Once every decade or so, the Nani-Bajou rouses from a slumber to sate its hunger. During those months-long orgies of blood and violence, the Ojibwe of Northern Ontario knew to avoid Miminiska Lake and the unfathomable creature that dwells within its dreary depths.

If an unknown lake monster should exist anywhere in Ontario, Miminiska Lake is the place. You can't get much farther from civilization than this large body of water, which is located in the province's far north and is engulfed by endless kilometres of trackless boreal forest. Indeed, it's so remote that there are no roads leading to it, meaning very few people have ever even seen its pristine waters, let alone spent any time paddling its length or exploring its shoreline. Furthermore, Miminiska Lake is part of the Albany River that flows into Hudson Bay, so any creature in the lake has the opportunity to migrate as food sources diminish.

The Nani-Bajou is elusive to the point of being practically invisible (indeed, its name means "mysterious monster"), but it has on occasion been spotted. In a 1947 article that appeared in the *Niagara Falls Evening Review*, a sportsman who was fishing in this remote region shared his experience. He described the beast as "a snake-like creature, over 50 feet [15 metres] in length, with a head and mane like a horse." This description—which sounds an awful lot like a plesiosaur—seems to mesh with First Nations lore and the accounts of the few other anglers, hunters and adventurers who have seen it.

Few have seen the Nani-Bajou, but it's out there, growing hungrier by the day, until one day it will no longer be able to ignore the pangs in its stomach and will awaken again. Its presence will cause chaos. Boats will sink, wildlife will vanish, and some people will never return home from a day on the water. Some will have you believe the rumours of Nani-Bajou are nothing more than tall tales, whereas others claim this ancient creature is terribly real and that those who venture out onto Lake Miminiska may possibly be condemning themselves to a watery grave.

## Serra

The early explorers of Canada's Atlantic seaboard encountered all manner of terrifying marine monsters, some large enough to threaten to sink the explorers' ships and strand them on alien shores. Sir Humphrey Gilbert (1539–83) was one of those explorers who, in addition to disease, foul weather, uncharted waters and lack of provisions, had to contend with a horrifying monstrosity while charting the New World.

On his second voyage to North America, Gilbert and crew ran afoul of a sea monster in the Grand Banks, off New-foundland. He describes it in his journal as "a very lion to our seeming, in shape, hair, and colour, not swimming after the manner of a beast by moving on its feet, but rather sliding upon the water with his whole body, excepting the legs, in sight, neither yet diving under, and again rising above the water, as the manner is of whales, dolphins, tunnies, porpoises, and all other fish...." The beast "yawned and gaping wide, with ugly demonstration of long teeth, and glaring eyes," then passed alongside the ship and "send forth a horrible voice, roaring or bellowing as doth a lion." Gilbert admitted it was a "strange thing" to see a "lion in the ocean sea, or a fish in the shape of a lion".

Some have identified this monster as a Serra, a mainstay of medieval bestiaries. A massive fish, sometimes as long as 90 metres, it was thought to have a mane like that of a lion and a serrated crest (or fins, depending on the account), which cuts through boats as it swims under or alongside them. Perhaps there's something to this story, as Gilbert's ship was later sunk with many hands lost. The Serra had attacked Gilbert for invading its territorial waters, sending dozens to watery graves in the depths of the North Atlantic Ocean.

## Saumen Kar

The Inuit of Canada's Arctic face the real dangers of weather and bone-numbing temperatures in the frigid lands they inhabit. In addition to these natural hazards, they were also threatened with a variety of fearsome fauna. Among them is the towering menace that is the Saumen Kar.

Also known as the Tornit, this hulking Inuit Bigfoot roams the frozen wastes of the Arctic, protected from the elements by a shaggy coat of pure white hair. Its black, simian face is fearsome to behold, made more so by the twin twisted horns that spiral out from atop its head. Including these horns, a Saumen Kar stands as much as 4 metres tall.

Saumen Kars are respected and feared by the Inuit as wise but terrifying spirits of the land. They are said to live and hunt either alone or in small family units, only killing what they need to eat. Though they subsist mostly on fish and seals, they will also eat muskox, caribou and even birds. Though not typically aggressive to humans, they will on occasion attack people and, with their massive strength, can almost effortlessly tear a man in two. The most dangerous are adolescent Saumen Kar. When a young Saumen Kar reaches a certain age, it flies into a fit of rage, mindlessly and savagely attacking anything in its path—seal, wolf, bear or human—and can only be calmed if told an entertaining story. There have also been many instances when the mysterious Saumen Kar has communicated with human shamans via telepathy, sharing valuable knowledge or cautionary tales.

If these giants exist in the tundra and ice of the north, one might ask, how come we've no recent reports? First, their natural camouflage make Saumen Kars almost invisible among the snow banks and ice fields of their frozen homes, especially if they remain motionless. And if by chance it is seen, a Sauman Kar can simply use its telepathy to wipe a man's memory clean so that the eyewitness forgets the encounter ever took place. Simply put, we don't have accounts of Saumen Kars because they choose not to make their presence known.

## Sidehill Gouger

An elusive beast is said to hide within the more remote forested hills of Ontario, retreating to the deepest wilderness after settlers pushed into the region in the late 19th century. The Gouger, a species of wild goat, is well adapted to living on hillsides. Legs on one side of their bodies are shorter than the legs on the opposite side, allowing them to walk on steep slopes and stand comfortably on sloped terrain to graze. This peculiar adaptation meant, however, that they could only walk in one direction around the hill; if forced to walk in the other direction, they would topple over.

Gougers were once more numerous than they are today, but when settlers first moved into the region they domesticated gougers to crossbreed them with sheep and goats so the sheep and goats could graze more easily on the hills that dominated their new homesteads. The gouger's numbers have dropped precipitously in the century since, largely thanks to over-hunting and the loss of habitat. On rare occasions, those venturing into remote, inaccessible hills might find a trail gouged into the slope by these elusive beasts as they endlessly circle it, or even catch a fleeting glimpse of the mysterious animal itself. Or so goes the tall tales told by old-timers, tongue firmly in cheek.

## Silver Cat

According to lumbermen huddled around pot-bellied stoves in logging shanties, sharing stories on a cold winter's night, the most fearsome animal in the Canadian wilds was not the wolf, whose mournful howls they could hear echoing through the barren forests. Nor was it the lynx, wolverine, cougar or even the black or grizzly bear. Real woodsmen knew the deadliest animal to stalk the deepest recesses of the Canadian wilderness was the Silver Cat.

At first glance, this ferocious predator could easily be mistaken for a mountain lion. Silver in colour, it is 136 kilograms of pure muscle, and like all cats, has retractable claws. Its primary vocalization is an ominous low growl, again similar to a mountain lion. But several adaptations set this bloodthirsty beast apart.

First, obviously, is its unusual coloration—a striking silver, almost like moonlight shimmering on freshly fallen snow. More ominous was the cat's 4-metre-long prehensile tail, a weapon even more deadly than its razor-sharp teeth and flesh-rending claws. The tail ends in a bony knob—flat on one end, spiked on the other. A silver cat perches high in a tree, unmoving and hidden among the foliage, waiting patiently for prey to pass by below. Striking with deadly suddenness, it would crush the creature's skull with the blunt side of its tail. Then, it impaled the victim on the spiked side and drew its victim up into the tree to be devoured.

Silver cats are arboreal, very rarely leaving the treetops. And for good reason; on the ground, they are said to be clumsy and slow. Thankfully, their numbers have apparently plummeted since lumbermen told frightening stories about them because nothing has been heard of silver cats for nearly a century.

## Snow Wasset

The early settlers and lumbermen of densely forested northern Ontario often spoke of Snow Wassets, frightening predators as white as snow and as large as the biggest bear. Though many feared these beasts, whose huge claws rent livestock and human alike in devastating nighttime assaults, the truth is that Snow Wassets were always extremely rare and spent much of the year in Labrador, only migrating to the Great Lakes and Hudson Bay region in winters.

Snow Wassets resemble an unholy amalgam of polar bear and massive viper, and they are hungrier and more vicious than 40 wolverines. In the summer, the fur of a Snow Wasset turns vibrant green, and they hibernate in cranberry marshes, perfectly camouflaged amidst the cranberry bushes. Their survival depends on this camouflage because in the heat of summer, they are sluggish and move about clumsily on stumpy legs. When the snow of winter comes, Snow Wassets lose these rudimentary legs and travel through the snow like eels in water, slithering with lightning speed through and above the snow. They hunt like sharks, stalking prey from below and then bursting up from the snow to drag down animals as large as moose. Though the lion's share of their diet consists of moose and deer, Snow Wassets will consume any prey they happen upon, including their favourite victims: humans.

Thankfully, these terrors are assumed to be extinct or have retreated to the farther regions of the inhospitable Labrador and Hudson Bay wildernesses. Or perhaps they only ever lived in lumber shanty stories.

## Splinter Cat

How often do we see trees that have been split or shattered, or have thick branches that have been broken off? Such violent damage is frequently the result of high winds, lightning, ice accumulation in winter or rot. Cryptozoologists will suggest that some breakage can also be attributed to Sasquatch, who have frequently been reported to break branches, topple trees and snap saplings. But the experienced logger and shantyman knows that much of the damage can be traced back to a single cause: the elusive Splinter Cat.

The Splinter Cat is a large feline, comparable in height and length to the mountain lion but far heavier, with a rotund body that brings to mind a well-fed wild pig. A bony protrusion graces the end of its short muzzle. Tremendously strong legs are required to enable this cat to move through the thick forests it calls home and to climb trees in search of food—primarily bees, the honey they produce, woodpeckers, squirrels and raccoons.

When hungry—and a Splinter Cat is almost always hungry—it will scamper up a tree and search its trunk for hollows that might contain food. Upon finding one, the cat uses it powerful legs to propel itself at the hole. The bony nasal protrusion splinters the tree or even snaps the trunk in half, allowing the ravenous animal to eat whatever is hidden within the hollow. Splinter Cats are so heavy that sometimes even thick branches give way under their weight, causing them to break off and crash to the forest floor.

While large, strong and undoubtedly fearsome in appearance, the Splinter Cat poses no threat to humans. In years past, it was found all over the timbered regions of Canada and the northeastern United States. Today, this rare beast may well be extinct. But, old-time lumberjacks will caution, the Splinter Cat is only ever active at night so a number of them may well still exist, unseen by humans in the depths of our vast forests.

## Terichik

Few can say with certainty what strange things might lie beneath the frozen tundra of Canada's north. Might a giant worm that bursts out of the ground like a geyser to attack and devour its prey be possible? The Inuit speak of the Terichik, a monstrous man-eating worm, measuring over 30 metres long and as thick as a beluga. The first Terichik was born to an Inuit couple, but they were so appalled by their hideous offspring that they cast it aside, leaving it to die in the snow. To the world's ever-lasting misfortune, a pregnant woman found the worm baby, felt sorry for it and nursed it back to health. When the Terichik had recovered, it repaid the kindness of its surrogate mother by devouring her and her unborn child. Ever since, the Terichik have lusted after human blood.

The Terichik burrows through the frozen earth with ease, cunningly stalking surface prey, which it can smell even when the worm is kilometres underground. They burst without warning from below, swallowing whole wolves, caribou, muskoxen and humans alike.

Most will say the Terichik is pure myth. But some Inuit might disagree explaining that their skill at the hunt might explain why so few people have reported seeing these monstrous worms in person—the creatures size up their prey and attack with brutal suddenness, leaving no survivors to carry the tale back to civilization.

## Turtle Lake Monster

Said to combine the most terrifying aspects of snakes and fish, the Turtle Lake Monster inhabits Turtle Lake, in Central Saskatchewan. Reports date back centuries, when the local Cree had a legend warning people not to venture into the monster's territory. Those Cree who saw it and survived claim that its hunger is at once ravenous and undiscriminating—it tears into the flesh of any prey, from a beaver to a moose to a human being—with jagged teeth and thrashes violently in the chaos it creates when attacking its prey.

Those who have seen the Turtle Lake Monster in modern times don't describe a creature anywhere near as bloodthirsty or predatory. Instead, it's described as elusive and shy. In physical appearance, the monster is usually said to measure 3 to 10 metres long with a dark, scaly hide and a head resembling a dog or a snake atop a long, slender neck. One man who saw the creature in recent years said that it surfaced near his boat: "Its head came up, its back came up and it sort of rolled over; we never saw the tail and its head looked like a seahorse."

Some have speculated the monster might represent a relic population of prehistoric plesiosaurs that have somehow adapted to the environs of a cold freshwater lake. Naysayers might suggest it's an unusually large sturgeon, a fish not native to these waters but that might have made its way into the lake from the North Saskatchewan and Turtle Rivers during years of high overflow.

The Turtle Lake Monster seems to be seen less frequently in recent years. Some might say that's because the beast never existed. Others might say it's because the brutality and efficiency with which the Monster attacks ensures that its prey rarely escapes to spread knowledge of its existence.

## Waheela

Imagine coming face-to-face with a snarling wolf as tall as a grizzly bear at the shoulder, all muscles and flesh-ripping teeth. Such a creature would be the stuff of which nightmares are made. And yet, there's a chance that such a monstrous creature truly exists in Canada's far north, a savage terror said to be a cross between a wolf and a bear, which ravages the sub-Arctic hinterlands.

The Waheela (sometimes referred to as Saberwolf) is a cryptid that is said to wander the trackless wastes and forbidden forests of the Northwest Territories and across the border into Alaska. Though similar to Arctic wolves in some respects—most notably the heavy coat of pure white fur both species sport—the Waheela has differences that are immediately noticeable. First, there's the size. Eyewitnesses report Waheela standing as much as 1.3 metres at the shoulder and having a stocky, heavily built frame that might weigh 500 pounds or more. Arctic wolves, in comparison, stand no more than one metre at the shoulder and are relatively lean, topping out at 80 kilograms.

In addition, the Waheela has a wider head than modern wolves, overly large feet and hind legs that are appreciably shorter than the front legs. Unlike modern wolves, Waheela do not live in large packs. Witnesses claim to see only one Waheela at a time, or perhaps only two or three at the most, so it is believed that these animals are either solitary creatures, coming together only to mate, or exist in small family units. Whereas First Nations Peoples were not afraid of wolves, the same cannot be said of the Waheela. In their legends they describe the creature as an evil spirit with supernatural powers and blame it for killing and decapitating people.

It has been proposed that the Waheela is actually an amphicyonid (commonly referred to as a bear dog), a large extinct terrestrial carnivore that inhabited North America during the Middle Eocene to the Early Pleistocene, from 46 to 1.8 million years ago. Although called Bear Dogs, they were actually more closely related to modern dogs than bears. Vicious and powerful predators, some amphicyonids weighed as much as 100 to 600 kilograms. In size, physical description and habits, amphicyonids do seem remarkably similar to accounts of the Waheela.